Brand Alchemy:

The Art + Science of Conscious Branding

Joi M Sears

AUTHOR'S NOTE

Dear Reader,

As I write these words, I am filled with gratitude for your journey into the pages of "Brand Alchemy." This book is a labor of love, crafted to inspire and empower you in your quest for conscious branding.

In these chapters, we'll delve into the transformative power of branding, drawing on the timeless metaphor of alchemy. Together, we'll uncover the secrets to infusing purpose, creativity, and innovation into your brand to create profound change.

Thank you for joining me on this journey of discovery. May the wisdom shared within these pages help you unlock your brand's full potential and make a lasting impact on the world.

In solidarity,

Joi M Sears

TABLE OF **CONTENTS**

Brand
[brand]

A brand is more than a name, logo, or product; it's the intangible essence that defines a business, resonates with its audience, and shapes its identity. It embodies the values, purpose, personality, and unique promise that sets a company apart in the hearts and minds of its customers.

A brand is the bridge between a business and its community, a source of trust, and the driving force behind a meaningful connection.

Alchemy
[al-kuh-mee]

Alchemy is an ancient and mystical art that seeks to transform the ordinary into the extraordinary, the base into the noble, and the mundane into the magical. It is both a spiritual and practical journey, often associated with turning lead into gold, but with deeper symbolic meaning.

In the context of branding, alchemy represents the process of creating a brand that transcends the ordinary, evokes deep emotions, and connects with its audience on a profound level. It is the art of turning a business into a brand that is not only successful but also transformative, inspiring, and purpose-driven.

CHAPTER 01

THE POWER OF PURPOSE-DRIVEN BRANDING

Branding is the powerful alchemy that transforms a business from a mere entity into a compelling, unstoppable force in the marketplace. It's much more than just a logo, color palette, or catchy tagline—it's the soul of your work, the narrative that distinguishes you from the crowd, and the covenant you create with your audience. It forms the foundation upon which your success is built, shaping perceptions, forging connections, and driving loyalty.

Yet, for those who dare to infuse their brand with purpose, the potential for transformation goes far beyond business viability. For creatives, conscious entrepreneurs, and non-profit organizations, branding becomes a conduit—a means to become not just more profitable but genuinely purpose-driven and profoundly impactful.

Imagine a brand that transcends the exchange of products or services for profit. Picture an entity that, through the power of branding, becomes a catalyst for positive change. Purpose-driven branding, in its essence, aligns your business or organization with a higher calling, a mission that goes beyond the bottom line. It's the recognition that your brand can be a force for good, a source of inspiration, and a vessel for social, environmental, or cultural transformation.

The benefits of purpose-driven branding extend far beyond the boardroom. They resonate with the hearts and minds of your audience, forging connections rooted in shared values and aspirations. It's about becoming a beacon for those who seek not just products or services but alignment with a cause, a movement, or a vision for a better world.

When your branding is infused with purpose, it transcends the transactional and enters the realm of the transformational. It becomes a tool for impact, enabling you to create meaningful change, inspire others to join your mission and build a community of like-minded individuals who share your values. It elevates your brand from a commodity to a cause, from a business to a movement, and from a simple choice to a heartfelt commitment.

In the chapters that follow, *we will delve deeper into the art and science of purpose-driven branding.* We will explore the components that make up this transformative force and provide practical guidance on how to infuse your brand with purpose. Whether you're a creative seeking to craft a brand that reflects your artistic vision, an entrepreneur driven to make a difference, or a non-profit organization committed to a noble cause, this journey will empower you to harness the extraordinary potential of purpose-driven branding.

The Art and Science of Branding

Think of branding as a harmonious blend of art and science. The artistic aspect of branding lies in the creative, emotional, and often intangible elements that give a brand its unique identity. It's the way your brand makes people feel, the stories it tells, and the experiences it delivers. This artistic dimension is what captures hearts and minds, turning casual consumers into "brand stans."

On the other hand, the scientific side of branding is grounded in data, psychology, and strategy. It's about understanding consumer behavior, market dynamics, and the ever-evolving landscape of your industry. Science helps you decode the nuances of consumer preferences and adapt your brand to meet their changing needs.

Together, the art and science of branding form a dynamic partnership that can propel your brand to new heights. Think of it as a symphony, with the artistic elements providing the melody and the scientific components providing the structure and rhythm. When these two facets are in harmony, your brand becomes a powerful force to reckon with.

The Essence of Branding

At the core of branding lies its ability to distill your business into a coherent and compelling narrative. A brand encapsulates who you are, what you stand for, and why you matter. It shapes perceptions, builds trust, and communicates your values to the world.

In a world flooded with options, branding acts as a North Star for consumers. It simplifies choices and reduces decision fatigue. Consider the iconic Apple logo—a simple apple with a bite taken out of it. It represents a complex web of innovation, design, and user experience. It's a symbol that instantly communicates a promise of creativity and innovation.

Or take Nike's "Just Do It" slogan. It's more than just a tagline; it's a rallying cry that speaks to the indomitable human spirit. It's a call to action that transcends sport and motivates individuals to push their limits.

Branding as a Competitive Edge

Great branding is more than just a way to identify your products or services; it's your ticket to standing out in an increasingly crowded marketplace. It has the power to take what might otherwise be a mere commodity and turn it into a coveted, must-have item. It can propel a local business onto the global stage, making it a household name. For nonprofit organizations, it has the potential to elevate a noble mission into one that is genuinely impactful, rallying supporters and driving meaningful change.

Consider, for a moment, the remarkable ascent of Tesla, the electric car company that dared to disrupt an industry long dominated by gasoline-powered vehicles. Tesla's success wasn't solely the result of sleek car designs or impressive engineering; it was a testament to the transformative potential of branding. Tesla didn't just create cars; it crafted an identity synonymous with sustainable transportation, cutting-edge technology, and a vision of a greener, more sustainable future.

Tesla's brand spoke to consumers on a deeply emotional level, tapping into their desires for innovation, environmental responsibility, and prestige. It went beyond selling cars; it sold a dream—a dream of a world where transportation didn't harm the planet, where driving was an exhilarating experience, and where technology made life better. In doing so, Tesla created a fiercely loyal customer base and a brand that stands as a symbol of progress and sustainability.

This is the power of branding as a competitive edge. It's about infusing your brand with a sense of purpose and vision that resonates with your audience, elevating your offerings from the *ordinary to the extraordinary*. In the chapters ahead, we will explore how you can harness this same power, whether you are a creative striving to express your artistic vision, an entrepreneur seeking to make a difference or a nonprofit organization with a mission to change the world. Your brand has the potential to not only stand out but to become a force for good and in doing so, to achieve remarkable success.

Beyond Profit: The Power of Purpose

While profitability is undoubtedly a critical aspect of business, it's no longer enough. Brands today are expected to stand for something more profound. Purpose-driven branding transcends mere profit and focuses on creating a positive impact.

Take a brand like Warby Parker, for instance. It's not just an eyewear company; it's on a mission to make vision care accessible to all. For every pair of glasses sold, Warby Parker donates a pair to someone in need. This purpose-driven approach has not only differentiated them in a crowded industry but has also fostered a sense of community among their customers.

Or consider the outdoor apparel brand, The North Face. They have made environmental sustainability a core part of their brand identity, pledging to reduce their carbon footprint and protect wild places. This commitment has resonated deeply with their audience and has led to both increased sales and a heightened sense of purpose.

Purpose-driven branding isn't just a feel-good initiative; it's a strategic move that can lead to increased profitability and long-term sustainability. Brands that stand for something beyond profit often enjoy stronger customer loyalty, command higher prices, and attract employees who are passionate about their mission.

In this book, we'll explore the intricate interplay between the art and science of branding. We'll delve into the psychology of consumer behavior, the strategies that turn casual consumers into devoted advocates, and the innovative approaches of brands that have disrupted their industries. We'll uncover the secrets of brands that have transcended profit and harnessed the power of purpose to make a positive impact.

Let's go on a journey into the world of branding, where the heart of branding beats with the power of purpose and where your brand has the potential not only to thrive but to truly matter.

CHAPTER 02
BRAND PURPOSE:
DEFINING YOUR BRAND'S WHY

W hat is the purpose of your brand? Why does it exist, beyond making money, selling products, or providing a service? Understanding and articulating your brand's purpose is a critical component of effective branding. A brand purpose goes beyond what your business does and how it does it – it's the deeper "why" that drives everything you do.

The Essence of Brand Purpose

In a world where countless brands fight for attention, the true essence of your brand lies in its purpose. It's the driving force behind your existence, the North Star, that guides your every move. Your brand purpose transcends the mundane objectives of profitability and market share; it embodies a higher calling.

Consider brands like Patagonia, where the purpose extends beyond selling outdoor apparel to a commitment to environmental sustainability and corporate social responsibility. This purpose-driven approach has not only set them apart in a crowded industry but has also created a passionate community of customers who share their values.

Or take TOMS, whose mission is to "improve lives through business." Their brand purpose isn't just about selling shoes; it's about making a positive impact on people's lives, one pair of shoes at a time.

The Role of Mission Statements

Your brand purpose serves as the foundation upon which you build your business. But how do you translate this purpose into a clear, compelling message that resonates with your target audience? That's where your mission statement comes into play.

A mission statement is a concise declaration that encapsulates the essence of your brand's purpose and what you aim to achieve. It should serve as a guiding light for your business, an inspiration for your team, and a promise to your customers.

When crafting a mission statement, consider these key factors:

Identify your purpose: Clearly communicate why your brand exists and what problem it aims to solve for your target audience.

Be specific and concise: Your mission statement should be brief and to the point, conveying the essence of your brand succinctly.

Use strong language: Craft your mission statement with powerful, clear language that conveys your passion and commitment.

Consider your audience: Write your mission statement with your target audience in mind, making sure it resonates and inspires them.

Be authentic: Ensure your mission statement aligns with your brand's core values and beliefs, representing who you are and what you stand for.

By adhering to these principles, you can create a mission statement that not only communicates your brand's purpose but also resonates with your audience and sets you apart from competitors.

The Vision Statement

Once your mission statement is in place, the next step is to craft a vision statement. While a mission statement defines your brand's purpose and objectives, a vision statement paints a vivid picture of what your brand aspires to achieve in the future.

Think of your vision statement as a compass guiding you and your team toward a shared goal. It should be clear, concise, and future-oriented.

To create a compelling vision statement, ask yourself:

• What kind of impact do we want to make in the world?

• Where do we see ourselves in five, ten, or twenty years?

• What are our long-term goals for our brand?

Your vision statement should be aspirational but also grounded in reality. It should motivate and inspire, something you and your team can strive towards.

Defining Brand Values

Brand values are the principles that shape your brand's identity and behavior. They reflect your company's culture, beliefs, and priorities, guiding decisions on communication and interaction with your audience.

Identify qualities and attributes that are important to your brand and customers, such as integrity, innovation, authenticity, diversity, excellence, or sustainability. Your brand values should be specific, meaningful, and relevant to your audience.

Once defined, ensure these values are consistently communicated across all brand touchpoints, from your website to customer service interactions. Brand values are not just buzzwords; they form the foundation of your brand's identity and guide daily decisions and actions.

Examples of Strong Brand Values

To inspire your own brand values, consider these examples from well-known brands:

- **Nike:** Prioritizes innovation, inspiration, sustainability, diversity, and inclusivity.

- **Patagonia:** Committed to quality, durability, and environmental stewardship.

- **Airbnb:** Values community, belonging, connection, diversity, and inclusivity.

- **Ben & Jerry's:** Focused on social justice, environmental sustainability, and fair trade.

- **Apple:** Emphasizes simplicity, creativity, innovation, privacy, and security.

These brands demonstrate how values can be integrated into identity and decision-making, creating authenticity and differentiation.

Crafting Your Brand Purpose

Now that the importance of brand purpose is clear, how can you craft one that resonates with your target audience? Here are steps to consider:

Identify Your Brand's Purpose:

- **Start with your why:** Reflect on what inspired your business and the problem you aim to solve.

- **Research your target audience:** Understand their needs and aspirations.

- **Analyze your competitors:** Find opportunities for differentiation.

Crafting Statements Aligning with Your Purpose:

- **Be concise:** Keep statements short, memorable, and clear.

- **Be authentic:** Reflect your true values and beliefs.

- **Be aspirational:** Inspire your team and customers to believe in a brighter future.

- **Be inclusive:** Show commitment to diversity, equity, and inclusion.

By following these steps, you can create a brand purpose that truly resonates with your audience, sets your brand apart, and guides your journey to success.

The Benefits of a Strong Brand Purpose

A strong brand purpose offers a range of benefits:

- **Builds brand loyalty:** When your purpose aligns with your customers' values, they become loyal advocates.

- **Differentiates from competitors:** It helps you stand out in a crowded market.

- **Attracts top talent:** It draws employees or collaborators passionate about your mission.

- **Drives business growth:** Purpose-driven brands tend to outperform competitors with higher customer loyalty and engagement.

Examples of successful brands with strong brand purposes include Patagonia, TOMS, Airbnb, and many more. In today's competitive landscape, a strong brand purpose is more crucial than ever. Define your brand's purpose, create statements that align with it, and communicate it to your audience. It could be the key to unlocking opportunities for your business, resonating with customers, and driving growth.

CHAPTER 03
**BRAND PERSONA:
UNDERSTANDING YOUR AUDIENCE
FROM THE INSIDE OUT**

I n the ever-evolving landscape of business, one fundamental truth remains unshaken: knowing your audience is paramount to success. Your audience is not an amorphous crowd but a diverse group of individuals, each with unique preferences, needs, and aspirations. To truly connect with them, you must go beyond surface-level demographics and delve into the intricacies of their lives.

This is where customer persona research comes into play. Customer personas, also known as buyer personas or audience personas, are fictional representations of your ideal customers. They embody the essence of your target audience, encapsulating their characteristics, behaviors, motivations, and more. Customer personas are not mere sketches but living, breathing profiles that guide your branding and marketing efforts with precision.

In this chapter, we embark on a journey of exploration and discovery. We will uncover the art and science of customer persona research, equipping you with the tools and insights to understand your audience on a profound level. From the techniques that allow you to listen to their voices directly to the analytical methods that reveal the hidden patterns in their behavior, we will walk through the entire process.

Effective customer persona research goes beyond statistics; it delves into the minds and hearts of your audience. It is the art of empathy, understanding the desires, fears, and aspirations that drive their choices. At the same time, it's a science - employing systematic methodologies to gather, analyze, and interpret data.

As you navigate this section, you will uncover best practices, actionable strategies, and real-world examples that illustrate the power of customer personas. Armed with this knowledge, you will be better equipped to tailor your branding and marketing efforts, forging meaningful connections that resonate with your audience on a personal level.

Understanding your target audience is the compass that guides your branding journey. To navigate this path effectively, you need a deep understanding of your audience's demographics, psychographics, behaviors, and preferences.

Demographics: Painting a Clear Picture

Demographics serve as the foundational framework for understanding your brand persona. Each demographic category provides a unique perspective on your target audience, allowing you to tailor your brand strategy more effectively.

For instance, knowing the age range of your audience is crucial because different age groups often have distinct preferences, behaviors, and communication styles. A brand targeting teenagers might prioritize vibrant visuals and social media engagement, while a brand targeting seniors may focus on more traditional marketing channels and ease of use.

Understanding the gender distribution within your audience can also guide branding decisions. A brand targeting a predominantly female audience might emphasize products or messages that resonate with women's needs and interests. Conversely, a brand with a more balanced gender distribution might aim for gender-neutral appeal.

Race and ethnicity are significant factors in today's diverse marketplace. Brands that acknowledge and respect various racial and ethnic backgrounds can foster inclusivity and resonate more deeply with their audience. For example, a brand embracing multiculturalism might feature diverse models in its advertising campaigns.

Income brackets provide insights into your audience's purchasing power. Brands targeting higher-income brackets might focus on premium products and experiences, while those catering to lower-income segments might prioritize affordability and value.

Geographic location helps you tailor your marketing efforts to regional preferences and cultural nuances. A brand seeking a global presence might adapt its messaging and product offerings to suit different markets.

Marital status and family composition inform brand decisions related to family-oriented products, services, or messaging. For instance, a brand catering to families with children might emphasize safety and convenience.

Occupational backgrounds and job titles offer insights into your audience's professional lives. A brand targeting entrepreneurs might highlight solutions that facilitate productivity or business growth.

Psychographics: Delving Deeper into Minds and Hearts

Psychographics delve into the complexities of your brand persona's values, beliefs, interests, behaviors, and attitudes. This deeper understanding enables you to craft a brand that resonates on a personal and emotional level.

Values and beliefs are the moral compass of your audience. Brands can align themselves with these principles, fostering trust and loyalty. For example, a brand emphasizing sustainability can attract environmentally conscious consumers.

Exploring goals reveals what your audience aspires to achieve. Brands can position themselves as facilitators of these ambitions. For instance, a fitness brand can align with the goal of a healthier lifestyle.

Interests offer opportunities for engagement and connection. Brands can create content and experiences that tap into these hobbies or passions. An outdoor gear brand can share adventure stories to captivate an adventurous audience.

Behaviors provide insights into daily routines and actions. Brands can cater to these routines by offering solutions that seamlessly integrate into consumers' lives. A skincare brand can emphasize ease of use for busy individuals.

Attitudes shape perceptions and decision-making. Brands can address these attitudes to influence preferences and loyalty. A brand promoting inclusivity can foster a welcoming community.

Needs and motivations uncover the "why" behind desires. Brands can identify these motivations and address them directly. For instance, a brand offering time-saving solutions can cater to customers' need for convenience.

Favorite Brands and Influences: Learning from Preferences

Exploring the brands and influences that resonate with your audience provides valuable insights into their preferences and aspirations.

Understanding favorite brands reveals the qualities and values that your audience appreciates. Brands can study these favorites to identify shared characteristics and incorporate them into their own identity.

Media consumption habits highlight where your audience seeks information and entertainment. Brands can use this information to select the most effective advertising channels and content types.

Purchase Behavior: Navigating Decision-Making

Examining how your brand persona makes purchasing decisions is critical for influencing their choices.

Identifying purchase factors allows brands to emphasize what matters most to their audience. Whether it's price, convenience, sustainability, or other factors, tailoring the offering to meet these criteria can drive sales.

Understanding the decision-making process itself—such as the stages consumers go through when considering a purchase—enables brands to align their marketing efforts with the customer journey. Brands can create content and strategies that support decision-making at each stage.

Communication Preferences: Crafting the Right Message

To effectively connect with your brand persona, it's crucial to understand how they prefer to consume information and what messages resonate with them.

Preferred communication channels are where your audience is most receptive to your brand's messages. Brands can allocate resources to these channels for maximum impact.

Messaging strategy involves tailoring brand messages to suit audience preferences. Some audiences may respond better to personal stories, while others might prefer data-driven content.

Content format refers to the style and length of content that appeals to your audience. Brands can create content that aligns with these format preferences, whether it's short videos, blog posts, or infographics.

By delving deep into demographics, psychographics, influences, purchase behavior, and communication preferences, brands can refine their understanding of their target audience and develop strategies that resonate on a personal level. This not only drives customer engagement but also fosters brand loyalty and long-term success.

Values, Attitudes, Lifestyles, and Behavior: Crafting a Holistic Persona

Lastly, weave together the collected information to craft a holistic brand persona. Understand the values they hold dear, their attitudes toward various aspects of life, the lifestyles they lead, and the behaviors that define them.

As you navigate this section, you will uncover best practices, actionable strategies, and real-world examples that illustrate the power of customer personas. Armed with this knowledge, you will be better equipped to tailor your branding and marketing efforts, forging meaningful connections that resonate with your audience on a personal level.

In this section, we'll take a look at three powerful research techniques that unveil the intricacies of your customer persona:

Exploring Customer Persona Research Techniques

User Interviews:

Imagine sitting across from your ideal customers, engaging in candid conversations that reveal their innermost thoughts and motivations. User interviews offer precisely that. By asking open-ended questions and fostering a conversational atmosphere, you can extract rich qualitative data directly from the source.

These insights delve into demographics, psychographics, needs, motivations, preferences, and behaviors, enabling you to comprehend your audience at a profound level. User interviews are a treasure trove of personal perspectives that illuminate the human side of your customer persona.

Surveys and Questionnaires:

Sometimes, you need to cast a wider net to capture the collective sentiments of your audience. Surveys and questionnaires are great tools for this. Well-structured surveys delve into the key aspects of your customer persona, covering demographics, interests, preferences, and purchase behavior. They allow you to reach a larger sample of your target audience, distributing your inquiries through diverse channels like email, social media, and your website. The analytical results provide statistical insights, unveiling trends and preferences among your audience. Surveys and questionnaires bring a quantitative dimension to your understanding of the customer persona landscape.

Social Media Analytics and Online Behavior Analysis:

In the digital age, your audience's footprint extends far beyond traditional surveys and interviews. Social media platforms and online behaviors offer a real-time glimpse into their world. Leveraging social media analytics and online behavior analysis tools empowers you to comprehend your target audience's digital interactions. These tools provide data on demographics, interests, online engagement patterns, and brand interactions. By monitoring social media conversations, tracking website analytics, and analyzing user-generated content, you gain a dynamic understanding of how your audience interacts with your brand and what content resonates with them. It's like peering into the digital mirror of your customer persona.

These three research techniques, whether used together or separately, form a powerful arsenal for building a comprehensive customer persona. They merge qualitative and quantitative data from direct interactions, surveys, and digital observations, ensuring you grasp the full spectrum of your audience's complexities. As we delve into each technique, you'll gain the insights and strategies needed to craft personas that not only inform your branding and marketing but also foster authentic connections with your audience.

Effective research is the cornerstone of creating accurate and insightful customer personas. To ensure the success of your research efforts, consider the following best practices:

- **Clearly Define Your Research Objectives:** Before embarking on any research, establish clear and specific goals. What do you want to learn about your target audience? What questions do you need to answer? Defining your objectives will guide your research process and keep it focused.

- **Mix Qualitative and Quantitative Methods:** A combination of qualitative and quantitative research methods provides a more comprehensive understanding of your customer persona. Qualitative methods like user interviews offer depth and context, while quantitative methods such as surveys provide numerical data for statistical analysis.

- **Select the Right Participants:** Ensure that your research participants represent your target audience accurately. Use demographic and psychographic criteria to recruit participants who match your ideal customer persona. This helps in gathering relevant and actionable insights.

- **Prepare Thoughtful Questions:** Craft well-thought-out questions for interviews and surveys. Open-ended questions encourage participants to share their thoughts and feelings, while closed-ended questions can provide specific data for analysis. Ensure that your questions cover all aspects of your customer persona, from demographics to behaviors.

- **Conduct User Interviews Skillfully:** When conducting user interviews, create a comfortable and non-judgmental environment for participants. Ask open-ended questions, listen actively, and encourage participants to elaborate on their responses. Avoid leading questions that may bias their answers.

- **Leverage Online Tools:** Use online survey and data analysis tools to streamline the research process. Platforms like SurveyMonkey, Google Forms, or TypeForm make it easier to distribute surveys and gather data efficiently. Additionally, social media analytics tools can help you monitor digital behavior.

- **Analyze Data Methodically:** When analyzing data, employ systematic methods. Organize and categorize responses, and look for trends and patterns. Consider using data visualization techniques like charts and graphs to make complex data more understandable.

- **Iterate and Validate:** Customer personas are not static; they should evolve with your business. Periodically revisit your personas to ensure they remain accurate and relevant. Validate your findings by comparing them with real-world results and customer feedback.

- **Share Insights Across Your Organization:** Make sure the insights gained from your customer persona research are shared across your organization. Your marketing, sales, product development and customer support teams can all benefit from a deep understanding of your target audience.

- **Maintain Ethical Research Practices:** Respect participants' privacy and data security. Clearly communicate the purpose of your research and obtain informed consent when necessary. Adhere to ethical guidelines and data protection regulations applicable in your region.

By following these best practices, you can conduct thorough and meaningful research to develop accurate and valuable customer personas that drive your branding and marketing strategies. Remember that understanding your audience is an ongoing process, and staying connected with them is key to maintaining effective customer personas.

By thoroughly researching and defining your brand persona, you create a powerful tool that not only informs your branding strategy but also empowers you to connect deeply with your target audience. In the next chapter, we will delve into the concept of brand personality, which adds an additional layer of depth to your brand's identity.

CHAPTER 04
BRAND PERSONALITY:
BREATHING LIFE INTO YOUR BRAND

In the world of branding, your brand is more than just a name or a logo; it's a living entity with a personality all its own. This brand personality is what sets you apart from the competition and shapes the way your audience perceives and connects with you. Just like people, brands possess distinct personalities that can attract, engage, and resonate with their audience on a profound level.

Understanding and harnessing the power of your brand's personality is not merely a marketing strategy; it's the key to forging deep and lasting connections with your customers. Your brand's personality is the bridge that allows your audience to relate to your values, aspirations, and vision. It's the emotional and psychological blueprint that underlies every interaction your audience has with your brand.

In this chapter, we'll embark on a journey to explore the captivating realm of brand personality. We'll dive into the intricacies of how your brand's personality influences perception, loyalty, and trust. While we won't delve into the specific framework of brand archetypes just yet, we'll lay the foundation for you to comprehend why brand personality matters profoundly in the branding landscape.

By the end of this chapter, you'll grasp the importance of honing your brand's personality and understand how it can be a driving force in creating meaningful and enduring relationships with your customers. So, let's embark on this exploration and uncover the profound impact of brand personality in the world of branding.

Why a Strong Brand Personality Matters

Imagine your brand as a person stepping into a crowded room. What kind of impression does it make? Is it warm and inviting, sparking conversations and drawing people in? Or does it stand aloof and distant, failing to connect on a meaningful level? Your brand's personality is the critical factor that determines how it's perceived and embraced by your target audience.

- **Building Trust and Relatability:** A well-defined brand personality fosters trust and relatability. When your brand exhibits traits that align with your audience's values and aspirations, it becomes relatable. This relatability forms the foundation of trust, a fundamental element of any successful brand-customer relationship.

- **Creating Emotional Connections:** Emotions play a central role in consumer decision-making. A brand with a strong personality has the power to evoke emotions, creating a deeper and more meaningful connection with its audience. When consumers feel an emotional attachment to your brand, they are more likely to choose it over competitors.

- **Setting You Apart:** In a sea of similar products and services, a distinctive brand personality sets you apart. It makes your brand memorable and recognizable, helping you stand out in a crowded marketplace. Consumers are drawn to brands that feel unique and authentic.

- **Consistency in Communication:** A defined brand personality serves as a guide for consistent communication. It ensures that every message, every piece of content, and every interaction with your audience aligns with your brand's character. Consistency breeds trust and clarity.

- **Appealing to Subconscious Desires:** Carl Jung's concept of archetypes taps into the subconscious desires and motivations of individuals. By aligning your brand with a specific archetype, you can tap into these hidden drives, making your brand more compelling and irresistible.

The Twelve Brand Archetypes

Carl Jung, the distinguished Swiss psychiatrist, delved into the intricacies of the human psyche and unearthed 12 universal archetypes. These archetypes serve as fundamental representations of various aspects of our collective unconscious. They reach into the depths of our shared culture and psychology, triggering emotions, desires, and motivations that have become deeply rooted in our understanding of the world.

Each of these archetypes possesses a distinct character and carries a unique narrative that resonates with the human experience. When you align your brand with one or more of these archetypes, you tap into a wellspring of profound emotions and connections. Your brand becomes a vessel for these timeless stories, making it not just memorable but deeply relatable to your audience.

By understanding and strategically harnessing these archetypes, you can craft a brand identity that evokes powerful emotional responses, fosters a sense of belonging, and leaves a lasting imprint on the minds and hearts of your customers. In the chapters that follow, we'll delve into each of these archetypes, exploring their traits, narratives, and how you can infuse them into your brand to create meaningful and enduring connections with your audience. So, let's embark on this journey of discovery, where the ancient wisdom of archetypes converges with modern branding to unlock the full potential of your brand's personality.

The Innocent: Optimistic, pure, and simple—the Innocent archetype embodies the childlike wonder and trust in a better world. Brands like Coca-Cola and Disney have successfully harnessed the Innocent archetype to convey happiness and nostalgia.

The Explorer: Adventurous, curious, and free-spirited—the Explorer archetype fuels the desire for discovery and new experiences. Brands like Jeep and National Geographic tap into this innate human urge for exploration.

The Sage: Wise, knowledgeable, and reflective—the Sage archetype represents a thirst for wisdom and understanding. Brands like Google and TED use this archetype to position themselves as authorities in their fields.

The Hero: Courageous, determined, and noble—the Hero archetype embodies the hero's journey, the triumph over adversity. Brands like Nike and Superman epitomize the Hero archetype, inspiring customers to be their best selves.

The Outlaw: Rebellious, provocative, and daring—the Outlaw archetype challenges the status quo and champions unconventional thinking. Brands like Harley-Davidson and Virgin embrace this rebellious spirit.

The Magician: Transformative, visionary, and intuitive—the Magician archetype represents the power to make dreams come true. Brands like Apple and Disney wield the magic of innovation and imagination.

The Regular Guy/Girl: Down-to-earth, friendly, and relatable—the Regular Guy/Girl archetype connects with everyday people, making them feel understood and valued. Brands like IKEA and Wendy's take this approach.

The Lover: Passionate, sensual, and romantic—the Lover archetype evokes deep emotional connections and desires. Brands like Victoria's Secret and Godiva cater to the passions of their customers.

The Jester: Playful, humorous, and irreverent—the Jester archetype injects joy and fun into the brand experience. Brands like Old Spice and M&M's use humor to captivate their audience.

The Caregiver: Compassionate, nurturing, and selfless—the Caregiver archetype embodies empathy and support. Brands like

Johnson & Johnson and UNICEF stand as pillars of care and responsibility.

The Creator: Imaginative, innovative, and expressive—the Creator archetype inspires creativity and self-expression. Brands like LEGO and YouTube empower their users to be creators.

The Ruler: Powerful, influential, and authoritative—the Ruler archetype exudes control and leadership. Brands like Rolex and Mercedes-Benz command respect and excellence.

In the pages that follow, we'll explore each of these archetypes in detail, offering insights into how they work, real-world examples of brands using them effectively, and how to select the archetype that best aligns with your brand's purpose and audience. By understanding your brand's personality archetype, you can craft a brand experience that resonates deeply with your customers, forging lasting connections and memorable brand experiences. Welcome to the world of brand archetypes—where your brand becomes a captivating character in the story of your success.

The Innocent:
Embracing Optimism and Simplicity

The Innocent archetype embodies the qualities of purity, simplicity, and optimism. Brands that adopt the Innocent persona often convey a sense of childlike wonder and an unwavering belief in the goodness of the world. They see the glass as half full and invite their audience to join them in embracing life's positive side.

Key Traits:

1. **Optimism:** Innocent brands radiate positivity and hope. They see challenges as opportunities and believe in the inherent goodness of people and the world.

2. **Simplicity:** These brands keep things uncomplicated. They value straightforwardness and clarity, making their offerings easy to understand and use.

3. **Purity:** The Innocent archetype is associated with purity, both in intentions and actions. These brands strive for transparency and honesty in all they do.

4. **Playfulness:** There's often a playful and lighthearted aspect to the Innocent brand. They approach life with a sense of fun and adventure.

5. **Trust:** Consumers are naturally drawn to Innocent brands because they exude trustworthiness and sincerity. There's a sense that these brands have nothing to hide.

Why Choose the Innocent Archetype?

If your brand aligns with the Innocent archetype, you're in a unique position to create an aura of trust, simplicity, and optimism around your products or services. By embracing these qualities, you can craft a brand personality that:

- **Attracts a Positive Audience:** Your optimistic outlook on life resonates with individuals seeking positivity and simplicity in their choices.

- **Builds Trust:** Your commitment to transparency and purity fosters trust, making customers feel secure in their relationship with your brand.

- **Creates Emotional Bonds:** The Innocent archetype taps into the emotional aspect of decision-making, forging deep connections with your audience.

- **Stands Out:** In a world often filled with complexity, an Innocent brand's simplicity sets it apart, making it memorable and relatable.

- **Inspires Joy:** Your playful approach to life and your brand can bring joy and happiness to your audience, making their experiences with your brand enjoyable.

Examples of the Innocent Archetype in Action

1. **Coca-Cola:** Coca-Cola's brand persona embodies the Innocent archetype with its emphasis on happiness, sharing, and optimism. The brand's classic "Open Happiness" campaign reflects its unwavering commitment to spreading positivity and joy.

2. **Disney:** Disney is a quintessential Innocent brand. Its commitment to storytelling, magic, and the belief in the goodness of humanity has made it a beloved and trusted brand for generations.

3. **Dove:** Dove's focus on purity and simplicity is evident in its "Real Beauty" campaign. The brand celebrates the natural beauty of individuals, promoting self-acceptance and authenticity.

Whether you're launching a new brand or revitalizing an existing one, embracing the Innocent archetype can help you create a brand personality that resonates with those seeking optimism, simplicity, and trust in their consumer choices. It's a powerful tool for crafting a brand that radiates positivity and fosters genuine connections with your audience.

The Explorer:
Embracing Adventure and Curiosity

The Explorer archetype embodies the qualities of adventure, curiosity, and a thirst for new experiences. Brands that adopt the Explorer persona often convey a sense of freedom and a desire to break free from the ordinary. They inspire their audience to embark on journeys, whether physical or metaphorical, in search of new horizons.

Key Traits:

1. **Curiosity:** Explorer brands are driven by an insatiable curiosity about the world. They encourage their audience to question, learn, and grow.

2. **Independence:** Independence and self-reliance are core values for Explorer brands. They value individuality and often celebrate the spirit of autonomy.

3. **Adventure:** Adventure is at the heart of the Explorer archetype. These brands inspire their audience to seek out new experiences and challenge the status quo.

4. **Open-mindedness:** Explorer brands are open to diverse perspectives and cultures. They embrace the idea that there's always more to discover.

5. **Fearlessness:** These brands often exhibit fearlessness in the face of the unknown. They encourage risk-taking and bold decision-making.

Why Choose the Explorer Archetype?

If your brand aligns with the Explorer archetype, you have the opportunity to create a brand personality that ignites a sense of adventure and curiosity in your audience. By embracing these qualities, you can craft a brand personality that:

Attracts the Adventurous: Your brand will naturally appeal to individuals who seek excitement and new experiences.

Inspires Exploration: You can inspire your audience to explore new horizons, whether it's trying new products, visiting new places, or embarking on personal journeys.

Fosters Independence: Explorer brands resonate with those who value independence and self-discovery, forging a bond with self-reliant consumers.

Cultivates an Open-minded Community: Your brand can become a hub for open-minded individuals who appreciate diverse perspectives and cultures.

Encourages Fearless Action: By embodying fearlessness, you can motivate your audience to take calculated risks and pursue their passions.

Examples of the Explorer Archetype in Action

1. **National Geographic:** National Geographic embodies the Explorer archetype by celebrating curiosity, adventure, and exploration. The brand inspires its audience to discover the world's wonders and embrace diverse cultures.

2. **GoPro:** GoPro is all about adventure and capturing life's most thrilling moments. The brand's products and content empower individuals to document their explorations and share their adventures with the world.

3. **Patagonia:** Patagonia's commitment to adventure and exploration is evident in its focus on outdoor apparel and environmental stewardship. The brand encourages its customers to embrace a life of outdoor adventure while championing sustainability.

Whether you're in the outdoor adventure industry or simply want to infuse your brand with a spirit of exploration, adopting the Explorer archetype can help you create a brand personality that resonates with those seeking adventure, curiosity, and a sense of independence. It's a powerful tool for crafting a brand that encourages exploration and fosters a community of like-minded adventurers.

The Sage: Embodying Wisdom and Knowledge

The Sage archetype represents wisdom, knowledge, and a deep understanding of the world. Brands that adopt the Sage persona convey a sense of thoughtful reflection and a commitment to learning. They inspire their audience to seek wisdom and make informed decisions.

Key Traits:

1. **Wisdom:** Sage brands are characterized by their wisdom and insight. They offer valuable guidance and encourage their audience to make thoughtful choices.

2. **Knowledge:** Knowledge is a cornerstone of the Sage archetype. These brands are dedicated to sharing information and fostering intellectual growth.

3. **Reflectiveness:** Sage brands encourage reflection and introspection. They value contemplation and self-awareness.

4. **Authority:** Brands with the Sage persona often have authority and expertise in their field. They are trusted sources of information.

5. **Problem-Solving:** Sages excel at problem-solving and helping their audience navigate challenges. They offer practical solutions and insights.

Why Choose the Sage Archetype?

If your brand aligns with the Sage archetype, you have the opportunity to create a brand personality that embodies wisdom and knowledge. By embracing these qualities, you can craft a brand personality that:

Builds Trust: Sage brands are trusted sources of information and guidance, which can foster trust and credibility among your audience.

Inspires Learning: Your brand can inspire a love of learning and personal growth in your customers, positioning you as a mentor and resource.

Fosters Reflection: Encourage your audience to pause, reflect, and make thoughtful choices, fostering a sense of mindfulness.

Demonstrates Authority: As a knowledgeable brand, you can establish authority and expertise in your industry, attracting those seeking reliable information.

Solves Problems: Sages excel at problem-solving, making your brand a valuable resource for addressing challenges.

Examples of the Sage Archetype in Action

1. **TED:** TED, known for its TED Talks, embodies the Sage archetype by sharing valuable knowledge and wisdom from experts across various fields. The brand encourages learning, critical thinking, and the exchange of ideas.

2. **Harvard University:** Harvard, as an institution of higher learning, epitomizes the Sage archetype. It represents the pursuit of knowledge, academic excellence, and intellectual growth.

3. **The New York Times:** The New York Times is recognized for its commitment to journalism and in-depth reporting. The brand serves as a trusted source of information and thoughtful analysis, embodying the Sage persona.

Whether you're in the education sector or aim to position your brand as a trusted source of knowledge and wisdom, embracing the Sage archetype can help you create a brand personality that resonates with those seeking wisdom, guidance, and a commitment to learning. It's a powerful tool for crafting a brand that inspires intellectual growth and fosters a community of lifelong learners.

The Hero: Embracing Courage and Noble Pursuits

The Hero archetype represents courage, determination, and the pursuit of noble causes. Brands that adopt the Hero persona inspire their audience to overcome challenges, embrace their inner strength, and strive for greatness. They are often associated with transformation and making a positive impact on the world.

Key Traits:

1. **Courage:** Hero brands are characterized by their courage to face adversity and take on challenges. They encourage their audience to confront obstacles with bravery.

2. **Determination:** Determination and a strong sense of purpose are core values for the Hero archetype. These brands inspire perseverance and commitment to noble goals.

3. **Idealism:** Hero brands often embody idealistic values and a vision of a better world. They inspire their audience to pursue noble causes.

4. **Leadership:** Brands with the Hero persona often exhibit leadership qualities. They lead by example and inspire others to follow their path.

5. **Impact:** Hero brands are driven by a desire to make a positive impact on individuals, communities, or the world. They encourage their audience to join them in their mission.

Why Choose the Hero Archetype?

If your brand aligns with the Hero archetype, you have the opportunity to create a brand personality that embodies courage, determination, and the pursuit of noble goals. By embracing these qualities, you can craft a brand personality that:

Inspires Action: Hero brands inspire their audience to take action and confront challenges with courage.

Fosters Determination: Encourage your audience to remain determined and focused on their goals, driving them toward greatness.

Champions Idealism: Hero brands are often associated with idealistic values and a vision of a better world, attracting individuals who share these aspirations.

Demonstrates Leadership: By leading by example, you can establish yourself as a leader in your industry or cause.

Makes a Positive Impact: Hero brands inspire individuals to join their mission and contribute to positive change.

Examples of the Hero Archetype in Action

1. **Nike:** Nike embraces the Hero archetype by inspiring individuals to push their limits, overcome challenges, and "Just Do It." The brand celebrates the athlete within and encourages everyone to pursue their goals fearlessly.

2. **The Red Cross:** The Red Cross represents the Hero archetype by providing humanitarian aid and saving lives in times of crisis. The brand's mission is to alleviate suffering and make a positive impact on communities worldwide.

3. **Elon Musk's SpaceX:** SpaceX embodies the Hero archetype by pushing the boundaries of space exploration and inspiring humanity to venture beyond Earth. The brand's ambitious goals inspire a sense of purpose and exploration.

Adopting the Hero archetype can help you create a brand personality that resonates with those seeking courage, determination, and the opportunity to make a positive impact on the world. It's a powerful tool for crafting a brand that inspires heroic actions and fosters a community of individuals committed to noble pursuits.

The Outlaw: Embracing Rebellion and Provocation

The Outlaw archetype represents rebellion, provocation, and the breaking of rules. Brands that adopt the Outlaw persona challenge the status quo, inspire non-conformity, and encourage their audience to question established norms. They are often associated with freedom, independence, and pushing boundaries.

Key Traits:

1. **Rebellion:** Outlaw brands are characterized by their rebellious spirit. They defy conventions and question authority, inspiring their audience to do the same.

2. **Provocation:** Provocation is a core element of the Outlaw archetype. These brands challenge the norm and provoke thought and action.

3. **Independence:** Brands with the Outlaw persona value independence and self-reliance. They inspire their audience to assert their individuality.

4. **Non-Conformity:** Non-conformity is a key theme for Outlaw brands. They encourage their audience to think differently and embrace uniqueness.

5. **Freedom:** The pursuit of freedom, whether personal, societal, or creative, is a central theme for Outlaw brands. They inspire their audience to break free from constraints.

Why Choose the Outlaw Archetype?

If your brand aligns with the Outlaw archetype, you have the opportunity to create a brand personality that embodies rebellion, provocation, and the quest for freedom. By embracing these qualities, you can craft a brand personality that:

Inspires Rebellion: Outlaw brands inspire their audience to challenge the status quo and question established norms.

Provokes Thought: Encourage your audience to think critically and consider alternative perspectives.

Values Independence: Celebrate independence and self-reliance, empowering your audience to assert their individuality.

Champions Non-Conformity: Outlaw brands promote non-conformity and uniqueness, fostering a sense of freedom.

Embodies Freedom: The pursuit of freedom can be a powerful motivator, attracting those who seek to break free from constraints.

Examples of the Outlaw Archetype in Action

1. **Harley-Davidson:** Harley-Davidson embodies the Outlaw archetype by celebrating freedom, rebellion, and the open road. The brand inspires individuals to embrace the spirit of adventure and independence.

2. **Apple (1984 Macintosh Ad)**: Apple's iconic "1984" Macintosh ad challenged the status quo and encouraged viewers to break free from conformity. It positioned Apple as a brand that values individuality and non-conformity.

3. **Red Bull:** Red Bull represents the Outlaw archetype by sponsoring extreme sports and pushing the boundaries of what is possible. The brand encourages individuals to embrace daring and unconventional pursuits.

Whether you're in the world of entertainment, extreme sports, or any industry that values rebellion, non-conformity, and freedom of expression, adopting the Outlaw archetype can help you create a brand personality that resonates with those seeking to challenge the norm and assert their individuality. It's a powerful tool for crafting a brand that inspires rebellion and encourages a sense of freedom and independence.

The Magician: Embracing Transformation and Innovation

The Magician archetype embodies transformation, innovation, and the power to make the impossible possible. Brands that adopt the Magician persona are visionary, inspiring, and have a deep sense of intuition. They are often associated with creativity, change, and a belief in the extraordinary.

Key Traits:

1. **Transformation:** Magician brands are masters of transformation. They take ordinary experiences and products and turn them into something extraordinary.

2. **Visionary:** A strong sense of vision is a hallmark of the Magician archetype. These brands inspire their audience with a glimpse of what's possible.

3. **Creativity:** Creativity and innovation are at the core of the Magician's identity. They see solutions where others see obstacles.

4. **Intuition:** The Magician relies on intuition and deep insight. They understand the hidden aspects of life and use this knowledge to create change.

5. **Belief in the Extraordinary:** Magician brands believe in the extraordinary and aim to make it a reality. They inspire their audience to believe in the impossible.

Why Choose the Magician Archetype?

If your brand aligns with the Magician archetype, you have the opportunity to create a brand personality that embodies transformation, innovation, and the power to make dreams come true. By embracing these qualities, you can craft a brand personality that:

Inspires Transformation: Magician brands inspire their audience to believe in the possibility of transformation and change.

Ignites Creativity: Encourage your audience to think creatively and embrace innovative solutions.

Shares a Vision: Share your brand's visionary outlook and inspire your audience to see the world in a new way.

Trusts Intuition: The Magician archetype trusts intuition and encourages others to do the same, fostering a sense of deep insight.

Believes in the Extraordinary: Embrace the belief that the extraordinary is possible, motivating your audience to pursue their dreams.

Examples of the Magician Archetype in Action

1. **Disney:** Disney embodies the Magician archetype by creating magical worlds and experiences. The brand inspires audiences of all ages to believe in the power of imagination and the extraordinary.

2. **Apple:** Apple's history of innovation and "think different" philosophy aligns with the Magician archetype. The brand encourages customers to embrace the transformative power of technology.

3. **Tesla:** Tesla is a modern example of the Magician archetype, as the brand pioneers electric vehicles and sustainable energy solutions. Tesla inspires a vision of a greener and more innovative future.

Whether you're in the world of entertainment, technology, or any industry that values transformation, innovation, and the belief in the extraordinary, adopting the Magician archetype can help you create a brand personality that resonates with those seeking change and innovation. It's a powerful tool for crafting a brand that inspires transformation and encourages a belief in the extraordinary.

The Regular Guy/Girl: Down-to-Earth and Relatable

The Regular Guy/Girl archetype represents brands that are approachable, down-to-earth, and relatable to the everyday person. These brands are not flashy or pretentious but rather embrace simplicity, friendliness, and a sense of belonging. They resonate with audiences seeking authenticity and a connection with relatable experiences.

Key Traits:

1. **Authenticity:** The Regular Guy/Girl archetype thrives on authenticity. These brands are genuine and transparent in their interactions.

2. **Approachability:** They are approachable and make customers feel comfortable like they're talking to a friend.

3. **Simplicity:** The Regular Guy/Girl archetype values simplicity and avoids unnecessary complexity or extravagance.

4. **Relatability:** This archetype connects with audiences by sharing common experiences and relatable stories.

5. **Friendliness:** Brands embodying this archetype are friendly and create a welcoming atmosphere for customers.

Why Choose the Regular Guy/Girl Archetype?

Choosing the Regular Guy/Girl archetype allows your brand to connect with customers on a personal level. It's a persona that thrives on realness and down-to-earth values. By embracing these qualities, you can craft a brand personality that:

Builds Trust: The Regular Guy/Girl archetype builds trust by being straightforward and relatable, fostering a sense of authenticity.

Creates Comfort: Customers feel comfortable and at ease with your brand, like they're among friends.

Simplifies Complexity: In a world of complexity, your brand simplifies things and makes them more approachable.

Fosters Relatability: Your brand shares common experiences with your audience, creating a sense of belonging.

Welcomes All: The Regular Guy/Girl archetype is inclusive and welcoming to all customers.

Examples of the Regular Guy/Girl Archetype in Action

1. **IKEA:** IKEA embraces simplicity and affordability, making well-designed home furnishings accessible to the everyday person. Their down-to-earth approach resonates with people worldwide.

2. **Subaru:** Subaru's "Love" campaign showcases the brand as approachable, family-oriented, and relatable. It's a brand that values authenticity and connection.

3. **Southwest Airlines:** Southwest Airlines positions itself as a friendly and approachable airline, creating a sense of camaraderie among passengers and employees.

Whether you're in the retail, travel, or service industry, adopting the Regular Guy/Girl archetype can help you build a brand personality that connects with audiences seeking authenticity, simplicity, and a sense of belonging. It's a powerful tool for creating a brand that feels like a trusted friend.

The Lover: Igniting Passion and Sensuality

The Lover archetype embodies passion, sensuality, and a deep connection. Brands that align with the Lover persona are often associated with desire, romance, and intimacy. They appeal to customers' emotions and create experiences that ignite passion and a sense of belonging.

Key Traits:

1. **Passion:** The Lover archetype is driven by passion and intense emotions. These brands evoke strong feelings and desires.

2. **Sensuality:** They embrace sensuality in their messaging, design, and overall brand experience, appealing to the senses.

3. **Connection:** The Lover archetype fosters deep connections with customers, creating a sense of intimacy and belonging.

4. **Desire:** Brands embodying this archetype are skilled at creating desire for their products or experiences.

5. **Romance:** Romantic themes and emotions are often intertwined with the Lover archetype.

Why Choose the Lover Archetype?

Choosing the Lover archetype allows your brand to tap into the power of emotions and desire. It's a persona that thrives on creating intimate connections with customers. By embracing these qualities, you can craft a brand personality that:

Ignites Passion: The Lover archetype ignites passion in your audience, creating intense emotional connections.

Appeals to the Senses: Your brand appeals to the senses, creating a multisensory experience.

Fosters Deep Connections: Customers feel deeply connected to your brand, fostering a sense of intimacy.

Generates Desire: The Lover archetype excels at creating desire for your products or services.

Embraces Romance: Brands under this archetype often infuse a touch of romance into their messaging and experiences.

Examples of the Lover Archetype in Action

1. **Victoria's Secret:** Victoria's Secret embraces the Lover archetype by creating an intimate and sensuous atmosphere for lingerie and beauty products. Their brand thrives on creating desire and passion.

2. **Godiva:** Godiva chocolates embody the Lover archetype, as they create a sensual and luxurious experience. Their brand appeals to the senses and fosters an emotional connection with chocolate lovers.

3. **Hallmark:** Hallmark infuses a touch of romance into its brand, celebrating love and meaningful connections. Their products and messaging evoke emotions and a sense of connection.

Whether you're in the fashion, luxury, or hospitality industry, adopting the Lover archetype can help you create a brand personality that ignites passion, appeals to the senses, and fosters deep emotional connections with your audience. It's a powerful tool for crafting a brand that resonates with those seeking passionate and sensory experiences.

The Jester: Playful, Humorous, and Irreverent

The Jester archetype embodies a sense of playfulness, humor, and irreverence. Brands that align with the Jester persona are known for their ability to make people laugh and not take life too seriously. They embrace a lighthearted and fun approach to engage their audience.

Key Traits:

1. **Playfulness:** The Jester archetype thrives on playfulness and humor. They inject fun into their brand personality.

2. **Humor:** Brands embodying this archetype have a knack for using humor effectively in their messaging and interactions.

3. **Irreverence:** They challenge conventions and often have a rebellious streak.

4. **Spontaneity:** The Jester archetype embraces spontaneity and doesn't stick to rigid rules.

5. **Lightheartedness:** Brands under this archetype maintain a lighthearted and carefree attitude.

Why Choose the Jester Archetype?

Choosing the Jester archetype allows your brand to entertain and engage with humor and lightheartedness. It's a persona that thrives on making people smile and laugh. By embracing these qualities, you can craft a brand personality that:

Entertains: The Jester archetype entertains your audience, making them laugh and brightening their day.

Engages Playfully: Your brand engages with a sense of playfulness, making interactions enjoyable.

Challenges Norms: This archetype isn't afraid to challenge conventions and break the mold.

Embraces Spontaneity: Brands under this archetype often take spontaneous and unexpected approaches.

Lightens the Mood: The Jester archetype brings a lighthearted and carefree spirit to your brand.

Examples of the Jester Archetype in Action

1. **M&M's:** M&M's characters, like the Red and Yellow ones, embody the Jester archetype with their playful and humorous antics. The brand uses humor effectively in its advertising.

2. **Old Spice:** Old Spice rebranded itself with a lighthearted and humorous approach, challenging traditional grooming product advertising with quirky and memorable commercials.

3. **Skittles:** Skittles takes a playful and often irreverent approach to marketing its colorful candies. Their campaigns are known for their unexpected and humorous twists.

Adopting the Jester archetype can help you create a brand personality that entertains, engages playfully, and challenges norms with humor and irreverence. It's a powerful tool for crafting a brand that brings smiles and laughter to your audience.

The Caregiver: Compassionate, Nurturing, and Selfless

The Caregiver archetype embodies compassion, nurturing, and selflessness. Brands that align with the Caregiver persona are driven by a desire to help, protect, and support their audience. They create a sense of safety and well-being, fostering a deep emotional connection.

Key Traits:

1. **Compassion:** The Caregiver archetype is characterized by compassion and empathy. They genuinely care about the well-being of their audience.

2. **Nurturing:** Brands embodying this archetype nurture and support their customers, providing a sense of comfort.

3. **Selflessness:** They prioritize the needs of others above their own, fostering trust and loyalty.

4. **Protection:** The Caregiver archetype often creates a feeling of safety and security for their audience.

5. **Support:** Brands under this archetype offer support, guidance, and assistance to those in need.

Why Choose the Caregiver Archetype?

Choosing the Caregiver archetype allows your brand to become a source of comfort and support for your audience. It's a persona that thrives on providing care and compassion. By embracing these qualities, you can craft a brand personality that:

Cares Deeply: The Caregiver archetype genuinely cares about the well-being of your audience.

Nurtures: Your brand nurtures and supports customers, creating a sense of comfort.

Builds Trust: This archetype's selflessness and protection foster trust and loyalty.

Provides Support: Brands under this archetype offer valuable support and assistance.

Creates Safety: The Caregiver archetype creates a feeling of safety and well-being.

Examples of the Caregiver Archetype in Action

1. **Johnson & Johnson:** Johnson & Johnson embraces the Caregiver archetype by providing a wide range of healthcare and personal care products. Their brand is associated with trust, care, and safety.

2. **UNICEF:** UNICEF embodies the Caregiver archetype through its mission to protect and support children around the world. The organization prioritizes the well-being of vulnerable populations.

3. **Dove:** Dove's Real Beauty campaign reflects the Caregiver archetype by promoting self-esteem and body positivity. The brand aims to support and empower women.

Whether you're in the healthcare, nonprofit, or personal care industry, adopting the Caregiver archetype can help you create a brand personality that cares deeply, nurtures, builds trust, provides support, and creates a sense of safety and well-being for your audience. It's a powerful tool for crafting a brand that makes a positive impact on people's lives.

The Creator: Imaginative, Innovative, and Expressive

The Creator archetype embodies imagination, innovation, and self-expression. Brands that align with the Creator persona are driven by a desire to bring new ideas and possibilities to life. They thrive on pushing boundaries, fostering creativity, and inspiring their audience.

Key Traits:

1. **Imagination:** The Creator archetype is characterized by a rich imagination and a passion for innovation.

2. **Innovation:** Brands embodying this archetype are at the forefront of creativity and innovation in their industry.

3. **Expressiveness:** They encourage self-expression and often celebrate individuality.

4. **Visionary:** The Creator archetype tends to be visionary, inspiring others with their ideas and possibilities.

5. **Boundary-Pushing:** Brands under this archetype often challenge conventional thinking and push boundaries.

Why Choose the Creator Archetype?

Choosing the Creator archetype allows your brand to inspire creativity, innovation, and self-expression in your audience. It's a persona that thrives on bringing new ideas to life. By embracing these qualities, you can craft a brand personality that:

Inspires: The Creator archetype inspires others with visionary ideas and possibilities.

Innovates: Your brand is at the forefront of creativity and innovation in your industry.

Celebrates Individuality: This archetype encourages self-expression and celebrates individuality.

Pushes Boundaries: Brands under this archetype challenge conventional thinking and push boundaries.

Fosters Creativity: The Creator archetype fosters creativity and imagination.

Examples of the Creator Archetype in Action

1. **Apple:** Apple embodies the Creator archetype by continuously pushing the boundaries of technology and design. Their brand is synonymous with innovation and creativity.

2. **LEGO:** LEGO encourages creativity and self-expression through its building blocks. The brand inspires children and adults alike to build and create.

3. **Adobe:** Adobe fosters creativity and self-expression through its creative software tools, empowering individuals and businesses to bring their ideas to life.

Whether you're in the technology, creative, or education industry, adopting the Creator archetype can help you create a brand personality that inspires, innovates, celebrates individuality, pushes boundaries, and fosters creativity and imagination. It's a powerful tool for crafting a brand that encourages innovation and self-expression.

The Ruler: Powerful, Influential, and Authoritative

The Ruler archetype embodies power, influence, and authority. Brands that align with the Ruler persona are driven by a desire to lead and make a significant impact in their industry or field. They exude confidence and command respect from their audience.

Key Traits:

1. **Power**: The Ruler archetype is characterized by a strong sense of power and authority.

2. **Influence:** Brands embodying this archetype have a significant influence on their industry or market.

3. **Confidence:** They exude confidence and a sense of control.

4. **Leadership:** The Ruler archetype is often seen as a leader and influencer.

5. **Visionary:** Brands under this archetype tend to have a clear and powerful vision for their future.

Why Choose the Ruler Archetype?

Choosing the Ruler archetype allows your brand to establish itself as a powerful and influential force in your industry. It's a persona that thrives on leadership and making a significant impact. By embracing these qualities, you can craft a brand personality that:

Commands Respect: The Ruler archetype commands respect and exudes confidence.

Leads: Your brand is seen as a leader and influencer in your industry or market.

Influences: This archetype has a significant influence on its audience.

Inspires Confidence: Brands under this archetype inspire confidence and a sense of control.

Sets a Vision: The Ruler archetype often has a clear and powerful vision for the future.

Examples of the Ruler Archetype in Action

1. **Rolex:** Rolex embodies the Ruler archetype by establishing itself as a powerful and authoritative luxury watch brand. It commands respect and exudes confidence.

2. **Forbes:** Forbes, a leading business publication, aligns with the Ruler archetype by providing authoritative and influential insights into the business world.

3. **Mercedes-Benz:** Mercedes-Benz exudes confidence and power in the automotive industry, positioning itself as a leader in luxury vehicles.

Whether you're in the luxury, leadership, or influential industry, adopting the Ruler archetype can help you create a brand personality that commands respect, leads, influences, inspires confidence, and sets a clear vision for the future. It's a powerful tool for crafting a brand that establishes itself as a significant and authoritative force.

CHAPTER 05
BRAND PROCLAMATION:
TELLING YOUR BRAND STORY

Your brand proclamation is the vital channel through which you communicate your brand story and message to your audience. It's the narrative that defines who you are, what you do, and why you matter. Crafting a compelling brand proclamation is the linchpin of a successful brand – one that resonates with your audience and motivates them to take action.

The Power of Storytelling

At the core of your brand proclamation lies storytelling, one of the most potent tools in your branding arsenal. Stories have an innate ability to captivate audiences and forge deep connections. They serve as bridges between the mind and the soul, resonating with us on profound levels. From ancient hieroglyphics to timeless fables, humans have shared stories for millennia.

Why Storytelling Matters?

Storytelling is woven into our very DNA. It's how we connect with one another and interpret the world around us. Stories are the bedrock of how we understand our place in the grand tapestry of existence, shape our identities, and impart social values. When we share stories, we delve into our shared human experiences, fostering a profound understanding of both our differences and similarities.

For entrepreneurs, storytelling is more than a skill; it's a superpower. It enables us to sell products, services, and ideas by connecting with our audience on a level that data alone can't achieve. Stories tap into our emotions and make us care. They allow us to convey our values, vulnerability, and humility. Through stories, we can communicate our messages authentically.

The Art of Crafting Your Brand Story

To create an effective brand proclamation, you must first comprehend your brand's purpose, persona, and personality. These foundational elements shape the narrative and messaging you'll employ. Your brand story should be authentic, compelling, and unforgettable.

Connecting with Your Audience

To connect with your audience effectively, understanding them is paramount. Delve into their desires, needs, and motivations. Uncover what makes them tick, what keeps them awake at night, and what ignites their aspirations. Your story should not only address their surface-level needs but also resonate with their deeper, often unspoken desires.

Crafting Your Brand Story

Your brand story is the heart of your brand proclamation, and it plays a pivotal role in conveying your brand's values, aspirations, and vision. The art of storytelling is about crafting a narrative that not only engages but also emotionally resonates with your audience, leaving a lasting impression. There are several types of brand stories, each with its unique power to connect with your audience:

Finding Your Why:

This brand story is a powerful way to connect with your audience on a deeply personal level. It reveals the moment when you discovered your "why" – the core reason behind your current path. Often, this "why" is driven by a profound lesson or personal transformation. Sharing this narrative allows your audience to glimpse into your journey of self-discovery and transformation. It humanizes your brand, making it relatable and inspiring. For example, a wellness coach might share the story of their personal health struggles, the moment they realized the importance of well-being, and how this revelation led them to their current mission of helping others achieve wellness.

Inventor's Journey:

This narrative is particularly compelling for brands and entrepreneurs who have developed innovative solutions to pressing problems. It recounts the problem you faced, which compelled you to invent or create a solution. The "Inventor's Journey" story showcases your entrepreneurial spirit, creativity, and problem-solving abilities. It highlights your brand's unique selling proposition – the innovative solution that sets you apart in the market. For instance, a tech startup might share the story of how they identified a gap in the market, faced the challenge head-on, and developed a groundbreaking technology that changed the industry landscape.

Lesson Learned:

This type of brand story is ideal for individuals in the education, coaching, or motivational speaking fields. It centers on a valuable lesson you've learned and now want to share with your audience. By sharing your personal growth journey and the insights gained along the way, you position yourself as a trusted guide and mentor. This narrative is not only relatable but also deeply inspirational, as it demonstrates your commitment to personal and professional growth. For instance, an author might share the story of how a life-changing book transformed their perspective and inspired them to become a writer, aiming to impact others with their knowledge and wisdom.

Incorporating these brand stories into your brand proclamation allows you to connect with your audience on a profound level. These narratives evoke empathy, inspire trust, and communicate your brand's authenticity. Ultimately, crafting your brand story is a journey of self-discovery and a means to inspire and engage your audience, forging a powerful connection that extends beyond a mere transaction. It's about sharing your unique journey, values, and aspirations, creating a brand narrative that resonates with the hearts and minds of your audience, and leaving an indelible mark in their memories.

Brainstorming Story Ideas

Everyone has a story to tell, and the most compelling narratives often emerge from the fabric of everyday life. You don't need to lead an extraordinary existence to craft a story that resonates deeply with your audience. In fact, it's the relatable stories, rooted in everyday struggles and triumphs, that often have the greatest impact. Here's how you can uncover and develop your brand story:

Start with Your Audience:

To discover the most resonant story for your brand, it's essential to begin with a deep understanding of your target audience. You're not just telling any story; you're crafting a narrative that speaks directly to their needs, desires, and aspirations. Start by identifying their pain points – the challenges they face, the problems they seek to solve, and the hurdles they encounter on their journey. By pinpointing these issues, you can create a story that addresses their most pressing concerns.

Uncover Their Desires:

While addressing pain points is crucial, it's equally important to tap into the unspoken desires and aspirations that your audience may harbor. What are the dreams and ambitions that drive them? What are the deeper longings that they may not readily express? Here's where you can employ a creative strategy by connecting these desires to the seven deadly sins – envy, greed, lust, sloth, gluttony, pride, or wrath. These primal human emotions and desires can serve as powerful motivators within your storytelling.

For instance, let's say you're a fitness coach. Your audience's pain points might include struggling to lose weight, lacking energy, and feeling self-conscious. By connecting these issues to their underlying desires, you can craft a story that resonates deeply. You might highlight the desire for envy (wanting to be the fittest person in the room), the longing for pride (feeling confident and proud of one's body), or the aspiration for lust (to feel attractive and desirable).

Align with Your Unique Value Proposition:

As you brainstorm story ideas, it's crucial to consider how your brand's unique value proposition intersects with your audience's desires. Your story should not only resonate with their emotions but also position your brand as the solution to their problems and aspirations. Your unique selling points should seamlessly align with the story you're telling, reinforcing why your brand is the ideal choice.

From Ordinary to Extraordinary:

Remember, extraordinary stories can emerge from the most ordinary circumstances. While you may not have faced extraordinary challenges, it's the human experience and relatability that make your story compelling. Your audience seeks authenticity, vulnerability, and a connection with a real person who understands their struggles and desires.

By brainstorming story ideas that empathetically address your audience's pain points, desires, and motivations while weaving in your unique value proposition, you can create a brand story that resonates profoundly. It's through this narrative that you can forge a powerful bond with your audience, demonstrating your understanding of their needs and your commitment to helping them achieve their aspirations. Storytelling becomes the conduit through which you connect with your audience on a profound level, making your brand not just relatable but genuinely transformative.

Story Structure

The Hook:

Your story's hook is like the headline of an article or the trailer of a movie. It's a single sentence that grabs your audience's attention and makes them stop in their tracks. The key here is to address their desires or pain points directly. Ask questions that resonate with their needs and desires. By using language that's relatable and engaging, you can entice your audience to lean in and continue reading or listening.

The Status Quo:

To make your story relatable, it's crucial to share the challenges and struggles you faced before embarking on your transformative journey. These struggles can be both internal and external. Describe what life was like, the obstacles you encountered, and the emotions you experienced. By painting a vivid picture of your "before" state, your audience can connect with you on a personal level. They'll see themselves in your story, making it more engaging and impactful.

The Trigger:

The trigger is the turning point or challenge that initiated your journey. It's the moment when you were presented with a choice or when an inciting incident changed the course of your life or business. This part of your story builds tension and curiosity, as your audience wonders how you'll respond to this critical moment. It's the juncture that sets the stage for the transformation to come.

The Big Idea:

Uncover the profound lesson or truth that you've learned throughout your journey. This is the core message that underpins your story and provides it with depth and meaning. Your big idea is the wisdom you've gained, the insight you've discovered, or the revelation that has shaped your life or business. It's the "aha" moment that often comes after overcoming challenges or embracing change.

The Transformation:

Share how you took that big idea and turned it into action. Describe the steps you took, the choices you made, and the actions you implemented to transform your life or business. Show your audience the journey you embarked on, the challenges you faced, and the milestones you achieved. This part of your story is about illustrating how you evolved from your "before" state to your transformed state.

The Impact:

Explain how your story has influenced not only your life but also the lives of others. Share the changes, improvements, or advancements that have occurred as a result of your transformation. Highlight the positive outcomes and the ripple effect of your journey. This is where you demonstrate the real-world impact of your story, making it relatable and inspiring for your audience.

The Call to Action:

In the final part of your story, clarify what's in it for your audience. How does your story relate to your unique value proposition? What action do you want your audience to take after hearing your story? Whether it's subscribing to your newsletter, purchasing your product, or joining your cause, make your call to action clear and compelling. Show your audience how they can benefit from your story and the value you offer.

By structuring your brand story using these components, you can create a narrative that not only engages your audience but also guides them on a journey of transformation and action. Your story becomes a powerful tool that resonates deeply, inspires change, and fosters a connection that goes beyond words.

Remember, Your Bio Isn't a Story:

One common pitfall in storytelling is turning it into a mere resume or biography. While it's essential to showcase your achievements and credentials, your brand story should transcend this. Instead of listing accolades and accomplishments, focus on the narrative arc of your journey. Stories have clear beginnings and ends, and your goal should be to connect emotionally with your audience, leading them to see the value in your product, service, or idea.

Write How You Talk:

Authenticity is key in storytelling. Write in a manner that mirrors how you speak in everyday conversations. Read your story aloud to ensure it flows naturally and resonates with sincerity. When your story sounds authentic, it becomes relatable and trustworthy. Your audience should feel like they're having a genuine conversation with you, not reading a scripted monologue.

Don't Tell, Show!:

Effective storytelling is about more than just conveying information; it's about creating an immersive experience. Instead of relying on descriptive adjectives alone, use vivid and sensory language to paint pictures with your words. Engage your audience's senses and emotions. By showing rather than telling, you invite your audience to step into your story and experience it firsthand. This approach makes your narrative more engaging and memorable.

Be Authentic and Vulnerable:

Authenticity and vulnerability are powerful tools in storytelling. Share your character flaws, moments of doubt, and challenges you've faced on your journey. Embrace vulnerability as a means of connecting on a deeper level with your audience. When you're open about your I

Imperfections and setbacks, you become relatable and human. Authenticity and vulnerability are the cornerstones of forming genuine connections with your audience.

Mastering the Art of Storytelling:

Storytelling is indeed your most potent entrepreneurial tool. It's a way to bridge the gap between your brand and your audience, transcending mere marketing and becoming a genuine, human connection. When you craft and share your brand's story authentically, you have the power to create profound connections and inspire your audience to take action. Storytelling isn't just about conveying information; it's about sparking emotions, driving engagement, and motivating your audience to become part of your brand's narrative.

By keeping these storytelling principles in mind, you'll be better equipped to craft narratives that resonate deeply with your audience and drive meaningful connections that go beyond transactional relationships. Your brand story becomes a source of inspiration, engagement, and loyalty.

Brand Voice: Your Brand's Unique Personality

Brand voice refers to the distinctive personality and style your brand conveys through its communication. It's the way your brand "speaks" to your audience. Developing a unique and consistent brand voice is crucial for building a recognizable and relatable brand. Here's how to define and implement your brand voice:

Personality Traits: Identify the personality traits that align with your brand and resonate with your audience. Is your brand friendly, professional, witty, or compassionate?

Audience Understanding: Tailor your brand voice to your target audience's preferences and expectations. Speak their language and adopt a tone they can relate to.

Consistency: Maintain a consistent brand voice across all communication channels, including social media, websites, marketing materials, and customer support. Consistency builds trust and recognition.

Guidelines: Develop brand voice guidelines that outline key characteristics, preferred language, and tone. Share these guidelines with your team to ensure a unified voice.

Brand Tone: Adapting to Context

While your brand voice serves as the foundational element of your communication, your brand tone acts like the emotional nuance or mood that you infuse into your messaging. Think of it as the specific flavor or attitude your brand adopts based on the situation or context. Here are some essential aspects to consider when it comes to brand tone:

Situational Adaptation: The ability to tailor your brand's tone to specific contexts and audiences is a valuable skill. For instance, when responding to customer support inquiries, your tone may lean towards being empathetic and understanding. In contrast, during a product launch announcement, your tone might take on an enthusiastic and confident demeanor. The key is to align your tone with the emotions and expectations of your audience in each scenario. This adaptability ensures that your brand remains relatable and resonates with diverse customer needs.

Empathy: One of the most powerful tools in your branding toolkit is an empathetic tone. Empathy can significantly enhance your relationships with customers. Show genuine understanding and compassion when addressing customer concerns or handling complaints. By acknowledging their feelings and experiences, you not only resolve issues but also build trust and loyalty. An empathetic tone communicates that your brand cares about its customers on a personal level.

Humor: Humor, when used appropriately, can be a potent tool for making your brand more approachable and memorable. However, it's essential to ensure that the humor you employ aligns with your brand's personality and values. Consider your target audience's sensibilities to avoid offending or alienating them. A well-placed joke or witty remark can make your brand stand out, but it should never come at the expense of professionalism or inclusivity.

Clarity: Maintaining clarity in your brand's tone is crucial, especially when conveying important information. In situations where precision is paramount, such as product specifications, terms and conditions, or safety instructions, it's essential to be straightforward and avoid ambiguity. A clear and concise tone ensures that your audience fully comprehends the message, reducing the likelihood of misunderstandings or confusion.

In summary, brand tone is the adaptable facet of your brand's communication that allows you to connect with your audience on an emotional level. By effectively modulating your tone based on the context, practicing empathy, using humor judiciously, and prioritizing clarity, you can create a dynamic and engaging brand persona that resonates with your audience in various situations. The ability to strike the right tone demonstrates your brand's versatility and responsiveness to customer needs, fostering deeper connections and brand loyalty.

Brand Messaging: Crafting Compelling Content

Brand messaging forms the core narrative that you convey to your audience. It's a comprehensive story that encapsulates your brand's values, mission, vision, and unique selling points. Crafting effective brand messaging is essential for connecting with your audience and building a strong brand identity. Here are some key elements and tips to consider:

Storytelling: Storytelling is a fundamental component of effective brand messaging. It allows you to weave your brand's story into your communication. Share the journey you've taken, including the challenges and successes that have shaped your brand's identity. Storytelling helps humanize your brand and makes it relatable to your audience. When crafting your brand story, consider using the classic storytelling structure with a beginning, middle, and end. Make it engaging, emotionally resonant, and reflective of your brand's values and personality.

Value Proposition: Your brand's value proposition is the cornerstone of your messaging. It's crucial to clearly and succinctly articulate what sets your brand apart from the competition and the value it offers to customers. Explain how your products or services solve specific problems or fulfill critical needs within your target audience. To create an effective value proposition, identify your unique selling points (USPs) and emphasize them in your messaging. Your value proposition should answer the question: "Why should customers choose your brand?"

Mission and Vision: Incorporating your brand's mission statement and vision into your messaging is a powerful way to convey purpose and direction. Your mission statement defines your brand's overarching purpose and why it exists beyond profits. It reflects your commitment to making a positive impact on the world. Your vision statement outlines your aspirations and long-term goals. Sharing these statements with your audience helps them understand the deeper motivations driving your brand. When crafting your mission and vision statements, ensure they align with your brand's values and resonate with your target audience's beliefs.

Customer-Centric Approach: Effective brand messaging should be customer-centric. Focus on how your brand directly benefits your customers. Address their pain points, challenges, and aspirations.

Highlight how your solutions or offerings meet their specific needs and provide valuable solutions. Tailor your messaging to address the unique concerns and desires of your target audience. Use language that speaks directly to them and demonstrates your brand's commitment to serving their best interests.

Consistency: Consistency is key when it comes to brand messaging. Ensure that your messaging aligns with your brand's core values, personality, and visual identity. Consistency across all communication channels, from your website and social media to marketing materials and customer interactions, helps reinforce your brand's identity and fosters trust and recognition among your audience.

Audience Research: Before crafting your brand messaging, conduct in-depth audience research. Gain a deep understanding of your target audience's demographics, psychographics, pain points, and preferences. This research will help you tailor your messaging to resonate with your audience on a personal level.

Effective brand messaging is about crafting a comprehensive narrative that encapsulates your brand's identity, values, and unique selling points. By incorporating storytelling, emphasizing your value proposition, sharing your mission and vision, and adopting a customer-centric approach, you can create messaging that resonates with your audience, fosters trust, and strengthens your brand identity. Remember that consistency and audience research are essential elements in ensuring that your messaging effectively connects with your target audience across all touchpoints.

Taglines: Memorable Brand Mantras

Taglines are powerful tools in the world of branding. They are short, memorable phrases that encapsulate the essence of your brand or convey your unique value proposition. Crafting an effective tagline is a critical step in brand development. Here are some key considerations and tips for creating taglines that leave a lasting impression:

Simplicity: The hallmark of a great tagline is simplicity. Keep it concise and easy to remember. Aim for brevity, as shorter taglines tend to be more memorable and impactful. A simple tagline is more likely to stick in the minds of your audience and become associated with your brand. Avoid long, convoluted phrases that are difficult to recall.

Clarity: Clarity is essential in tagline creation. Your tagline should communicate a clear and unmistakable message about your brand's identity or promise. It should leave no room for ambiguity or confusion. A well-crafted tagline succinctly conveys what your brand stands for and what it offers to customers. When developing your tagline, consider the core values, mission, or unique selling points that define your brand.

Uniqueness: To stand out in a crowded marketplace, it's crucial to craft a tagline that is unique and distinctive. Avoid generic phrases and clichés that have been overused in your industry. Your tagline should set your brand apart and pique the curiosity of your audience. Think creatively and explore fresh angles that capture the essence of your brand in a novel way.

Relevance: A great tagline should align seamlessly with your brand's core values or mission. It should feel like a natural extension of your brand identity. When developing your tagline, consider how it relates to the products or services you offer and the promises you make to your customers. Ensure that it resonates with your target audience and reinforces your brand's authenticity.

Emotion: Taglines have the power to evoke emotions and connect with your audience on a deeper level. Consider how your tagline can trigger specific emotions or sentiments that align with your brand's personality and values. Whether it's excitement, trust, inspiration, or nostalgia, a well-crafted tagline can elicit a powerful emotional response from your audience.

Testing and Refinement: Creating the perfect tagline often involves a process of testing and refinement. Don't be afraid to brainstorm multiple tagline options and gather feedback from peers, colleagues, or focus groups. Test the resonance of your tagline with your target audience to ensure it strikes the right chord. Be open to making adjustments and iterations until you find the tagline that truly encapsulates your brand.

Taglines are memorable brand mantras that distill your brand's essence into a few words. By prioritizing simplicity, clarity, uniqueness, relevance, and emotion in your tagline creation process, you can develop a powerful and enduring tagline that resonates with your audience, reinforces your brand identity, and sets you apart from the competition. Remember that crafting the perfect tagline may require time and creative exploration, so don't rush the process.

Headlines: Grabbing Attention

Headlines are your brand's first point of contact with your audience, serving as powerful hooks that can draw readers or viewers into your content. They are the gateway to your brand's messaging and storytelling. Crafting effective headlines requires careful consideration of several key elements:

Relevance: Effective headlines directly address the reader's interests or pain points. They should immediately convey why the content is valuable to the audience. Whether it's solving a problem, fulfilling a desire, or providing valuable information, relevance is paramount.

Clarity: A clear headline leaves no room for ambiguity. It should clearly and concisely communicate the central message or value proposition of the content. Avoid vague or convoluted language that might confuse or deter your audience.

Emotion: Headlines have the power to evoke curiosity, emotion, or a sense of urgency, all of which can engage the reader's or viewer's interest. Consider how your headline can tap into the emotional aspects of your brand's messaging, making it more compelling and memorable.

Consistency: Headlines should align seamlessly with your brand's voice and messaging. Consistency in tone, style, and messaging across all your content reinforces your brand identity and helps build trust with your audience. Ensure that your headlines reflect your brand's personality and values.

Conciseness: In a world of information overload, concise headlines are more likely to grab and hold the audience's attention. Keep headlines succinct, avoiding unnecessary words or filler. Every word in your headline should serve a purpose and contribute to its impact.

Elevator Pitches: Quick Connections

Elevator pitches are brief, persuasive descriptions of your brand that can be delivered in the time it takes to ride an elevator. They are essential for making quick and memorable connections with your audience, whether you're networking, presenting, or engaging in casual conversation. Effective elevator pitches should:

Convey Essence: Summarize the core essence of your brand in a sentence or two. This essence should capture what makes your brand unique and why it matters. Think of it as the distilled heart of your brand's identity.

Engage: Elevator pitches should be engaging and attention-grabbing. They should spark curiosity and interest in your brand. Consider starting with a thought-provoking question, a surprising fact, or a bold statement that piques the listener's curiosity.

Highlight Benefits: Emphasize what sets your brand apart from the competition and the value it brings to customers. Your elevator pitch should leave a lasting impression by focusing on the benefits and solutions your brand provides.

Tailor to Audience: Adapt your elevator pitch to different audiences or contexts. While the core essence remains the same, you can emphasize different aspects of your brand depending on who you're speaking to. Tailoring your pitch shows that you understand your audience's needs and interests.

By mastering the art of crafting compelling headlines and elevator pitches, you empower your brand with the tools to effectively communicate its message, capture attention, and make memorable connections. These elements play a crucial role in your brand's overall messaging strategy, reinforcing its core essence and driving engagement with your target audience.

CHAPTER 06
BRAND POSITIONING:
DISCOVERING YOUR DISTINCTIVE SPACE

B rand positioning is a strategic journey that goes beyond mere recognition—it's about defining your brand's unique space in the market and orchestrating how your target audience perceives you. To craft an effective brand positioning strategy, you must have a profound understanding of your audience, know your competition inside and out, and leverage your brand's distinctive qualities. Here's a detailed exploration of this critical aspect of branding:

Introduction: Crafting Your Unique Brand Positioning

In the ever-evolving marketplace, where countless brands vie for consumers' attention, the ability to stand out and leave a lasting impression is paramount. This is where brand positioning comes into play, offering you a strategic toolkit to carve out your distinct identity amidst the noise.

Brand positioning is not merely a marketing buzzword; it's the cornerstone of your brand's success. It defines how your business distinguishes itself in a crowded field, allowing you to attract the right audience, communicate your uniqueness, and showcase the inherent value behind your products or services.

Imagine your brand as a star in a constellation, each one shining with its unique brilliance. Brand positioning is the compass that guides you to your precise point in the sky, ensuring you don't get lost amidst the vastness of the cosmos. It's about aligning your brand with a strategic direction that resonates with your vision, values, and, most importantly, your audience's needs.

In this section, we delve deep into the art and science of brand positioning, unveiling five major strategies to set your brand apart. Each strategy represents a different path to success, and the one you choose will profoundly influence your brand's messaging, image, and impact. Whether you're inclined towards prioritizing exceptional customer service, unrivaled convenience, top-tier quality, daring differentiation, or unbeatable pricing, your chosen positioning strategy will guide your journey toward brand success.

The strategy you select should seamlessly align with your brand's mission, values, and long-term vision. It's not just about standing out; it's about doing so in a way that authentically represents your brand and appeals to your target audience. So, embark on this exploration of Brand Positioning Strategies, and discover how to position your brand for unrivaled success in today's competitive marketplace.

Customer Service:

Customer service as a brand positioning strategy revolves around providing exceptional service experiences that address common pain points in a human-centered way. Here's a more detailed exploration:

Understanding Pain Points: In this approach, your brand's first task is to thoroughly understand the pain points, challenges, and frustrations your target audience faces. Conduct in-depth customer research to identify these pain points and determine how your products or services can provide effective solutions.

Fast and Reliable Service: The cornerstone of this strategy is offering swift and dependable service. Respond to customer inquiries promptly, resolve issues efficiently, and ensure that your customer support team is well-trained and empowered to deliver top-notch service.

Personalized Interactions: Elevate the customer service experience by personalizing interactions. Tailor your support and assistance to the unique needs of each customer. Show empathy, actively listen, and make customers feel valued and understood.

Consistency: Consistency in delivering high-quality customer service is essential. Maintain a uniform level of service excellence across all touchpoints, whether it's through live chat, phone support, email correspondence, or in-person interactions.

Feedback Loop: Establish a feedback loop that allows customers to share their experiences and suggestions. Act on this feedback to continuously improve your customer service and adapt to changing needs.

Convenience:

Convenience as a brand positioning strategy is all about making your products, services, and experiences exceptionally user-friendly and accessible. Here's a more comprehensive look:

Streamlined Processes: Optimize your business processes to minimize friction for customers. Ensure that every step, from browsing your website to making a purchase, is intuitive and efficient.

Accessibility: Make your offerings accessible to a wide audience. This could involve providing multiple payment options, offering digital accessibility features, or even having physical locations in strategic areas.

Ease of Use: Focus on creating products or services that are straightforward and easy to use. User-friendly interfaces, clear instructions, and intuitive designs should be a priority.

Digital Presence: Leverage digital platforms and technology to enhance convenience. Offer online ordering, digital customer support, and mobile apps to cater to the evolving needs of tech-savvy consumers.

Location and Timing: If applicable, consider physical location and operating hours. Being in the right place at the right time can significantly contribute to convenience. For example, 24/7 customer support or strategically located physical stores.

Quality:

Quality as a brand positioning strategy revolves around offering premium, high-quality products or services that create a VIP experience for customers. Here's a more detailed breakdown:

Premium Materials and Craftsmanship: Invest in premium materials and craftsmanship to ensure that your products or services stand out in terms of quality. This could include using the finest materials, implementing strict quality control processes, and partnering with skilled artisans.

Exclusivity: Position your brand as exclusive, catering to a select clientele who value and appreciate top-tier quality. Limited editions, bespoke offerings, and unique features can enhance this sense of exclusivity.

Exceptional Customer Experience: Quality extends beyond the product itself; it includes the entire customer experience. From the moment a customer interacts with your brand to post-purchase support, every touchpoint should reflect excellence.

Pricing Reflects Quality: High quality often comes at a premium price. Be transparent about the value customers receive for the price they pay. Emphasize that your brand provides a superior and luxurious experience.

Reviews and Testimonials: Use customer reviews and testimonials to showcase the exceptional quality of your offerings. Genuine feedback from satisfied customers can be a powerful testament to your brand's commitment to quality.

Differentiation

Differentiation as a brand positioning strategy emphasizes being innovative, unique, and divergent in your approach. Here's a more in-depth exploration:

Innovative Solutions: Continuously seek innovative solutions to industry challenges or customer pain points. Position your brand as a thought leader and trendsetter by introducing groundbreaking products or services.

Unique Methodology: Develop a unique methodology or approach that sets your brand apart from competitors. This could be a proprietary technology, a distinct design philosophy, or a revolutionary process that enhances your offerings.

Creative Branding: Use creative branding and storytelling to convey your brand's divergence. Craft a narrative that highlights your brand's willingness to break conventions and challenge the status quo.

Bold Vision: Communicate a bold and visionary outlook for your industry or niche. Your brand should inspire customers with a sense of limitless possibilities and a commitment to pushing boundaries.

Consistent Uniqueness: Maintain consistency in your brand's distinctiveness. Ensure that every aspect of your brand, from product design to marketing campaigns, aligns with your unique identity.

Pricing

Pricing as a brand positioning strategy revolves around offering products or services at a significantly lower cost than competitors. Here's a more detailed examination:

Cost Efficiency: Streamline your operations and processes to achieve cost efficiency. Identify areas where you can reduce expenses without compromising on quality or service.

Value Proposition: Communicate your value proposition clearly. Emphasize how your lower prices translate to savings for customers without sacrificing product quality or service standards.

Price Match Guarantees: Consider offering price match guarantees to instill confidence in customers. This assures them that they're getting the best deal while enjoying the benefits of your brand.

Volume Discounts: Implement volume discounts or loyalty programs that reward repeat customers or those who make larger purchases. These incentives can further drive savings for your target audience.

Transparent Pricing: Maintain transparency in pricing. Avoid hidden fees or unexpected charges. Customers should feel confident that your brand offers straightforward and affordable solutions.

By selecting one or a combination of these brand positioning strategies, you can effectively set your brand apart from competitors, create compelling messaging, and emphasize the unique value your brand provides to customers. This strategic approach ensures that your brand resonates with your target audience and entices them to engage with your products or services.

Scrutinize the Competitive Landscape

Understanding your competition is not just about identifying who they are but also about comprehending their strategies, strengths, and weaknesses. Conduct a comprehensive competitive analysis:

Competitor Offerings: Scrutinize the products or services offered by your competitors. What features, qualities, or benefits set them apart? What are their core strengths and vulnerabilities?

Messaging and Branding: Analyze their brand messaging, positioning, and visual identity. What emotions or values do they invoke in their audience? How do they express their brand personality? Identify gaps and opportunities for differentiation.

Customer Perception: Investigate how customers perceive your competitors. What do they appreciate about them? Are there pain points or areas where competitors fall short, according to customer reviews and feedback?

Market Trends: Stay attuned to industry trends and emerging technologies. Identify areas where your brand can lead, innovate, or introduce fresh perspectives.

Discover Your Unique Selling Proposition (USP)

Your Unique Selling Proposition (USP) is the crux of your brand positioning. It encapsulates what sets your brand apart and why customers should choose you over competitors. Discover your USP through these steps:

Identify Strengths: Conduct an honest evaluation of your brand's strengths. Consider factors like exceptional quality, innovative features, exemplary customer service, or specialized expertise. What advantages can you confidently claim?

Niche Focus: Contemplate the possibility of narrowing your focus to a specific niche or segment within your market. Catering to a niche can make it easier to stand out, as you can become an expert and address unique needs more effectively.

Innovation: Explore opportunities for innovation and disruption within your industry. Can you introduce something groundbreaking, whether it's a new product feature, a more sustainable process, or an entirely fresh approach to an existing problem?

Craft Your Brand Positioning Statement

A well-crafted brand positioning statement encapsulates your brand's essence and what it offers to your audience in a concise yet impactful manner. It is the compass guiding your brand's journey. A compelling brand positioning statement should include:

What You Offer: Describe your product or service in clear terms. Explain how it addresses a specific problem or fulfills a need in your market.

Your Target Audience: Define your ideal customers or clients. Who are they, and what are their unique characteristics and preferences?

Your Differentiator: Highlight what distinguishes you from your competitors. What is your USP, and why is it valuable to your audience?

The Problem You Solve: Specify the problem or need that your brand addresses. What challenges do your customers face that your brand can resolve?

The Desired Perception: Outline how you want your target audience to perceive your brand. What emotions or associations should your brand evoke?

The Promise You Make: Explain the value and benefits customers can expect from your brand. What positive outcomes can they anticipate from choosing your brand over alternatives?

For instance, a brand positioning statement might read: "For environmentally conscious urban dwellers, our sustainable, handcrafted bicycles provide an eco-friendly and stylish transportation solution, offering a guilt-free commute and a greener future."

Consistency Is Key

Once you've articulated your brand's unique positioning, consistency is paramount. Every touchpoint with your audience should reinforce the key messages and values encapsulated in your positioning. A consistent brand experience builds trust, fosters recognition, and establishes your unique position in the market.

Monitor and Adapt

Market dynamics evolve, and consumer preferences shift. Regularly monitor your brand's performance, collect customer feedback, and stay attuned to market trends. Be prepared to adapt your positioning strategy to remain relevant and responsive to changing customer needs.

By following these steps and crafting a clear, compelling brand positioning, you can create a brand that not only stands out but also deeply resonates with your target audience. Your brand will establish a strong and lasting presence in the market, effectively distinguishing itself from competitors and delivering value that aligns with your audience's desires and expectations.

CHAPTER 07
BRAND PRESENCE:
CRAFTING A VISUAL IDENTITY
THAT ECHOES YOUR BRAND

Your brand presence is the visual embodiment of your brand, the visual language that communicates your essence to the world. It encapsulates elements like your logo, color palette, typography, imagery, and other design components that form a harmonious and distinguishable brand identity. Building a compelling brand presence involves a meticulous blend of creativity, strategy, and adherence to best practices in the field. Here's a comprehensive exploration of this crucial aspect of branding.

The Significance of a Creative, Comprehensive, and Cohesive Brand Identity

Your brand presence is your visual identity, the face of your brand that your audience recognizes and connects with. It's the first impression you make, the lasting image you leave, and the promise you convey. In a world brimming with choices, a creative, comprehensive, and cohesive brand identity is not merely a luxury; it's a necessity for success. Here's why:

Creativity That Captivates

Creativity is the spark that ignites curiosity and makes your brand memorable. It's what sets you apart from the ordinary and makes you extraordinary. A creative brand identity doesn't just follow trends; it sets them. It doesn't blend in; it stands out. Creativity infuses life into your brand, making it dynamic and engaging.

Think of iconic brands like Apple, Nike, or Coca-Cola. Their creative approach to branding has not only made them instantly recognizable but also deeply ingrained in our culture. A creative brand identity captures the essence of your brand and communicates it visually in a way that resonates with your audience's emotions and aspirations.

Comprehensiveness That Tells Your Whole Story

A comprehensive brand identity leaves no room for ambiguity. It's a visual narrative that tells your brand's story in vivid detail. It encompasses your logo, color palette, typography, imagery, and every visual element that represents your brand. It's not just about having a logo; it's about having a logo that encapsulates your brand's values, mission, and personality.

Consider Starbucks, for example. Their comprehensive brand identity includes not just the iconic mermaid logo but also the earthy color palette, the rustic typography, and the warm, inviting store designs. It's this comprehensive approach that creates a holistic brand experience, inviting customers to immerse themselves in the Starbucks story.

Cohesion That Builds Trust

Cohesion is the glue that holds your brand identity together. It ensures that every visual element aligns seamlessly with your brand's essence and purpose. A cohesive brand identity is recognizable across all touchpoints, from your website to your packaging, from your social media profiles to your physical storefront.

Cohesion breeds trust. When your audience sees a consistent brand identity, it reassures them that your brand is reliable and dependable. It tells them that you pay attention to the details and take your brand seriously. Cohesion builds brand recognition, making it easier for customers to identify and choose your brand in a crowded marketplace.

Consider the golden arches of McDonald's or the distinctive red of Coca-Cola. These brands have mastered the art of cohesion, making them instantly recognizable anywhere in the world. When you see those colors and symbols, you know exactly what to expect, and that consistency breeds trust and loyalty.

In essence, a creative, comprehensive, and cohesive brand identity is not just a visual asset; it's a strategic imperative. It's the bridge that connects your brand's purpose, persona, and personality with your audience's hearts and minds. It's the visual alchemy that transforms your brand from ordinary to extraordinary. So, as you embark on the journey of crafting your brand presence, remember that creativity, comprehensiveness, and cohesion are your most potent allies.

The Logo: Your Brand's Visual Icon

Your logo is the silent ambassador of your brand. It's the visual shorthand that speaks volumes about who you are, what you do, and why you matter. When people see your logo, it should trigger an immediate recognition of your brand and evoke the emotions and perceptions you want to convey. Here's why your logo is so crucial and some tips for designing one that truly represents your brand.

Why Your Logo Matters

Your logo is often the first point of contact between your brand and your audience. It's the image that appears on your website, your business cards, your social media profiles, and your products. It's the face of your brand, and as the saying goes, first impressions matter.

Immediate Recognition: A well-designed logo ensures that your brand is easily recognizable. It's the visual cue that triggers a memory of your brand, whether it's a swoosh, an apple with a bite taken out, or golden arches. These logos are so iconic that they need no introduction.

Emotional Connection: Your logo should not just be aesthetically pleasing; it should also evoke the right emotions. The Nike swoosh, f for example, conveys a sense of movement, energy, and aspiration. The Apple logo is sleek, innovative, and forward-thinking. Your logo should do the same for your brand.

Professionalism: A professionally designed logo signals that your brand is serious and reliable. It tells your audience that you pay attention to detail and that you're invested in your brand's image. A sloppy or amateurish logo can have the opposite effect.

Timelessness: A great logo should stand the test of time. It should be just as relevant and impactful decades from now as it is today. Think about logos like Coca-Cola or IBM; they've remained largely unchanged for years, and that consistency has contributed to their enduring success.

Tips for Designing Your Logo

Now that you understand the importance of your logo, here are some tips to keep in mind when designing one:

Simplicity: Keep it clean and uncomplicated. Memorable logos are often simple and easy to recognize. Avoid clutter and overly intricate designs. Think about the simplicity of the Apple logo or the FedEx arrow hidden within its lettering.

Relevance: Ensure your logo is closely tied to your brand's purpose, persona, and personality. It should visually represent what your brand stands for. For example, if you're an eco-friendly brand, your logo might incorporate elements of nature or sustainability.

Scalability: Your logo should look just as good on a business card as it does on a billboard. Test it at various sizes to ensure it remains legible and impactful. A logo that loses its clarity when scaled down loses its effectiveness.

Versatility: Consider variations of your logo for different applications and backgrounds. For instance, a simplified version for monochrome printing ensures it remains recognizable in all contexts.

Timelessness: Aim for a design that won't succumb to the trends of the moment. While it's essential to stay relevant, your logo should have a timeless quality that transcends fads. Think about how the Coca-Cola logo has remained virtually unchanged since the late 19th century.

Uniqueness: Your logo should set you apart from competitors. Avoid clichés and generic designs that blend in. Instead, strive for a logo that stands out and captures your brand's distinctiveness.

Remember that your logo is an investment in your brand's future. It's worth taking the time and resources to get it right because a powerful logo can be a catalyst for brand recognition, trust, and loyalty.

Color Palette: Communicating Emotions

Colors are powerful communicators. They have the ability to evoke emotions, create associations, and convey messages without words. When it comes to your brand, the colors you choose play a pivotal role in shaping how your audience perceives and connects with your identity. In this section, we explore the significance of color palettes in your brand presence and provide guidance on how to create an effective one.

The Psychology of Colors

Before delving into the practical aspects of creating a color palette, it's essential to understand the psychology of colors. Different colors can evoke a wide range of emotions and associations. For instance:

Red: Often associated with passion, energy, and excitement. It can also symbolize danger or urgency.

Blue: Conveys trust, reliability, and calmness. It's frequently used by tech companies and financial institutions.

Green: Represents growth, health, and nature. It's commonly linked to eco-friendly and sustainable brands.

Yellow: Evokes feelings of happiness, optimism, and warmth. It can also grab attention and signify caution.

Purple: Associated with luxury, creativity, and spirituality. It's often used by beauty and wellness brands.

Black: Symbolizes sophistication, elegance, and power. It's a popular choice in luxury branding.

Understanding these associations can help you select colors that align with your brand's values, personality, and message. Consider the emotions you want your brand to evoke and choose colors that resonate with those feelings.

Consistency Is Key

Consistency is the cornerstone of a strong brand identity. When it comes to your color palette, maintaining consistency across all brand materials is crucial. Your audience should instantly recognize your brand through its colors. To achieve this:

Establish Primary and Secondary Colors: Define a set of primary colors that represent your brand's core identity. These colors will be prominently featured in your logo, website, and marketing materials. Additionally, create a set of secondary colors that complement the primaries and offer versatility in design. Secondary colors can be used for backgrounds, accents, or to add variety to your brand visuals.

Provide Guidelines: Once you've chosen your primary and secondary colors, establish clear guidelines on how they should be used. Specify color codes (HEX, RGB, CMYK) for both digital and print applications. This ensures that your colors remain consistent across different media.

Test for Accessibility: Accessibility is an essential consideration, especially for web design. Ensure that your color choices meet accessibility standards, making your brand inclusive and user-friendly for all.

Flexibility for Varied Needs

While consistency is vital, it's equally important to have flexibility in your color palette. Different situations may require variations to accommodate diverse design needs. Here's how to achieve flexibility:

Primary vs. Secondary Colors: As mentioned earlier, primary colors represent your brand's core identity and should be used for branding elements like logos and headlines. Secondary colors can be reserved for backgrounds, accents, or secondary content.

Backgrounds and Accents: Consider creating color variations that work well as background colors or accents. These variations should harmonize with your primary and secondary colors while providing visual contrast when needed.

Monochrome Versions: Develop monochrome or grayscale versions of your logo and branding materials. This ensures your branding remains effective in black and white or in situations where color printing is limited.

Seasonal or Campaign Colors: For special occasions, seasons, or marketing campaigns, you can introduce temporary colors that align with the theme while still maintaining your core brand palette.

By striking a balance between consistency and flexibility, you'll have a color palette that not only reflects your brand's identity but also adapts to various design requirements and contexts. This versatility ensures your brand remains visually engaging and relevant in diverse scenarios.

Typography: Choosing Your Brand's Voice

Typography plays a vital role in defining your brand's voice and conveying its personality. It's the written language of your brand and impacts how your audience perceives your messages. In this section, we delve into the significance of typography in your brand presence and offer guidance on selecting the right fonts.

Readability Is Paramount

The foundation of effective typography is readability. Your chosen fonts should be easy to read, whether your audience encounters them on a billboard, website, or printed material. Here are some key considerations:

Platform Versatility: Your typography choices should work seamlessly across various platforms, including digital screens and print materials. Test your fonts in different sizes and formats to ensure legibility.

Consistency Enhances Brand Identity

Consistency in typography reinforces your brand identity. When you maintain a cohesive font system, your audience can recognize your brand more easily. Here's how to achieve consistency:

Font Pairing: Choose a primary font and a complementary secondary font. These fonts should align with your brand personality and values. The primary font is typically used for headlines and prominent text, while the secondary font complements it for body text and other content.

Style Definition: Establish clear guidelines for font styles within your brand. Define font sizes, weights (bold, regular, italic), and styles (serif, sans-serif) for various use cases. This creates a uniform look and feel across all your brand materials.

Establish a Clear Hierarchy

Typography helps you establish a visual hierarchy in your content. This hierarchy guides readers through your message, making it easier to read and comprehend. To create a clear text hierarchy:

Font Size: Use font size strategically to differentiate between headlines, subheadings, body text, and captions. Larger font sizes typically indicate more critical information.

Font Weight: Adjust the weight of your fonts to emphasize specific content. Bolder fonts can draw attention to important points or headings, while lighter weights can distinguish secondary text.

Font Style: Utilize font styles like italics or underlining sparingly for emphasis. These styles can be effective for highlighting specific words or phrases.

A well-thought-out typography system not only enhances the readability of your content but also reinforces your brand's visual identity. It's a crucial aspect of your brand presence that should align with your brand persona and personality.

By prioritizing readability, maintaining consistency in font choices, and establishing a clear text hierarchy, you'll create a typographic system that enhances your brand's voice and reinforces its unique identity across all communication channels.

Imagery: Conveying Your Brand's Narrative

Imagery is a powerful storytelling tool that shapes how your audience perceives your brand. Whether you're using photographs, illustrations, or graphics, the visuals associated with your brand carry significant weight. In this section, we explore the importance of imagery and provide guidance on making the most of it in your brand presence.

Imagery's Role in Brand Storytelling

Imagery serves as the visual language that communicates your brand's narrative. It's a window into your brand's world, offering insights into its values, personality, and mission. Here's why imagery matters:

Relevance: Every image you choose should align seamlessly with your brand's values and messaging. Whether it's a photograph or an illustration, the visual content should resonate with your target audience, reinforcing your brand's identity.

Consistency: Consistency in your visual content is key to fostering brand recognition. Maintaining a uniform style and tone in your imagery helps establish a strong and memorable visual identity. This could involve using specific filters for photographs or adhering to a particular illustration style.

Originality: Whenever possible, opt for original and unique imagery. Custom visuals set your brand apart and add authenticity to your storytelling. While stock photos can be useful, they might lack the uniqueness that custom visuals bring to the table.

The Visual Storytelling Continuum

Consider imagery as part of a continuum in visual storytelling. From your logo to marketing materials to social media posts, each piece of visual content contributes to your brand narrative. Here's how to make the most of imagery:

Logo and Brand Elements: Your logo is the visual icon that represents your brand at its core. It should encapsulate your brand's essence and be instantly recognizable. Additionally, other brand elements like icons and symbols should complement your logo, maintaining a cohesive visual identity.

Marketing Collateral: Imagery on marketing materials, such as brochures, flyers, and banners, should align with your brand's messaging and values. Use visuals that enhance your narrative and draw the audience in.

Website and Social Media: Consistency in imagery across your website and social media platforms is essential. Visuals on these channels should be not only relevant to your brand but also tailored to your target audience. Share content that resonates with your followers and reinforces your brand identity.

Content Creation: Whether you're producing blog posts, videos, or other content, your imagery should enhance the message. Use visuals that support your storytelling and engage your audience.

Imagery is a dynamic aspect of your brand presence that can captivate your audience, evoke emotions, and convey your brand's narrative effectively. By selecting relevant, consistent, and original imagery, you'll create a visual identity that reinforces your brand's message and resonates with your audience.

Visual Elements: Cohesion and Unity

Creating a cohesive and unified brand presence involves more than just the usual suspects like logos, colors, typography, and imagery. Visual elements like patterns, icons, and graphics play a significant role in maintaining consistency and reinforcing your brand identity. In this section, we'll explore the importance of these visual components and how they contribute to a unified brand presence.

Customization for Unique Branding

One way to stand out in a crowded marketplace is by developing custom visual elements that are uniquely yours. These elements can take the form of custom patterns, icons, or illustrations that align perfectly with your brand's values and personality. Customization not only sets you apart but also adds depth and authenticity to your brand presence.

Establishing Design Guidelines

Consistency in visual branding is crucial, and that's where design guidelines come into play. These guidelines serve as the rulebook for how visual elements should be used. They cover essential aspects such as spacing, proportions, and usage rules for all visual elements. By having clear design guidelines, you ensure that your brand maintains its visual integrity across all touchpoints.

Creating a Cohesive Visual Identity

A harmonious and cohesive visual identity is a powerful tool in brand recognition. When all your visual elements adhere to the same style and theme, your brand presence becomes instantly recognizable. Consistency in visual design fosters trust among your audience, as they come to associate your brand with reliability and professionalism.

Consistency Across Touchpoints

Your brand presence should maintain consistency across all touchpoints, whether it's your website, social media profiles, packaging, or marketing materials. Consistency isn't just about using the same logo; it extends to colors, typography, imagery, and all visual elements. This consistent presentation helps build trust, ensures recognition, and reinforces a strong brand image.

Adaptability and Evolution

Brands evolve over time, responding to changing market trends and customer preferences. Your brand presence should be adaptable to these shifts while retaining core elements that make your brand recognizable. When making updates or changes, it's essential to ensure that they align with your brand identity and resonate with your target audience.

A Living Visual Identity

Think of your visual identity as a living entity that grows and adapts with your brand. It's not static but dynamic, evolving in tandem with your brand's journey. Your brand presence is a reflection of your brand's story, and as your story unfolds, so should your visual identity.

In summary, custom visual elements, clear design guidelines, a cohesive visual identity, consistency across touchpoints, and adaptability to change are essential components of a robust brand presence. These elements work together to create a visual identity that not only stands out but also effectively communicates your brand's values and personality.

Seek Professional Guidance: Elevating Your Brand Presence

Collaborating with a professional graphic designer or branding agency can be a game-changer when it comes to refining your brand presence. Their expertise and experience can ensure that your visual identity aligns seamlessly with your brand identity and adheres to industry best practices. Here are some valuable tips for finding and working with a designer or agency:

1. **Define Your Needs:** Before you start searching for a designer, clearly define your brand's needs and goals. Are you looking for a complete brand overhaul or specific design work like a logo or website? Knowing your requirements will help you find a designer with the right expertise.

2. **Do Your Research:** Take the time to research designers or agencies that specialize in your industry or have a portfolio that resonates with your brand's style. Look for examples of their previous work to ensure they can deliver the quality and style you're seeking.

3. **Check Reviews and Testimonials:** Read reviews and testimonials from past clients to gauge the designer's professionalism, communication skills, and ability to meet deadlines. Positive feedback from satisfied clients is a good indicator of a designer's reliability.

4. **Review Portfolios:** A designer's portfolio is a window into their creative abilities and style. Look for diversity in their portfolio to ensure they can adapt to your brand's unique needs while maintaining a consistent level of quality.

5. **Communicate Your Brand:** During your initial discussions, be transparent about your brand's purpose, persona, and personality. A good designer will want to understand your brand's story and values to create a visual identity that truly represents your essence.

6. **Set Clear Expectations:** Clearly communicate your project's scope, timeline, and budget. Establishing these expectations upfront ensures that both you and the designer are on the same page, minimizing misunderstandings later on.

7. **Ask Questions:** Don't hesitate to ask questions about the designer's process, creative vision, and how they plan to achieve your brand's goals. A professional designer should be able to explain their approach clearly.

8. **Collaborate Actively:** Be an active participant in the design process. Provide constructive feedback and be open to the designer's suggestions. Collaboration can lead to the best results.

9. **Trust the Process:** Remember that professional designers have a wealth of knowledge and experience. Trust their expertise and be open to their creative input while ensuring it aligns with your brand's vision.

10. **Evaluate the Results:** Once the project is complete, evaluate the results against your initial goals and expectations. Assess whether the brand presence created effectively conveys your brand's values, personality, and unique selling points.

Working with a professional designer or agency can be a worthwhile investment in ensuring that your brand presence not only captivates your audience but also leaves a lasting impression. Their guidance and creative input can elevate your brand's visual identity, align it with industry best practices, and set you on the path to greater success. A well-crafted brand presence is a powerful tool for conveying your brand's essence and forging meaningful connections with your audience.

Shaping Your Brand Presence

In the ever-evolving landscape of business and branding, your brand presence stands as a beacon, guiding your audience toward a deeper understanding of who you are and what you represent. It's the visual, emotional, and intellectual bridge between your brand identity and the hearts and minds of those you aim to serve. Through creativity, comprehensiveness, and cohesion, your brand presence communicates your values, personality, and unique selling points, leaving an indelible mark on your audience.

Creativity is the spark that ignites the flames of curiosity and engagement. It's the force that allows you to break free from the ordinary, to stand out in a sea of sameness. Whether it's in the design of your logo, the choice of colors, the typography, or the imagery, creativity infuses life and energy into your brand presence.

Comprehensiveness ensures that no detail is left unattended. It's the comprehensive approach that makes your brand presence a holistic experience, from the logo to the color palette, typography, imagery, and even the visual elements. It ensures that every visual touchpoint resonates with your brand's values, making your message consistent and trustworthy.

Cohesion is the glue that binds it all together. It's the common thread that unites your brand's visual elements, creating a harmonious symphony that your audience can easily recognize and identify with. Cohesion is the secret sauce that makes your brand presence memorable and unmistakable.

Remember that your brand presence isn't static; it's a dynamic force that should evolve with your brand's growth and changing goals. Be ready to adapt while staying true to the core elements that make your brand unique and recognizable.

By focusing on these principles and adhering to best practices, you have the power to create a brand presence that captivates, resonates, and leaves an indelible mark on your audience. It's a journey of creativity, strategy, and authenticity that leads to the creation of a visual identity that not only represents your brand but also forges a deeper connection between you and those you serve. Your brand presence is your voice in a noisy world, your visual handshake, and your lasting impression—so make it count.

CHAPTER 08
**BRAND PERFORMANCE:
NURTURING REMARKABLE
BRAND EXPERIENCES**

I n the ever-evolving landscape of business and marketing, the importance of delivering an exceptional brand experience cannot be overstated. Brand performance is the heartbeat of your business, setting the stage for how your audience interacts with and perceives your brand. It encompasses every touchpoint, from the moment a potential customer discovers your brand to their post-purchase experience.

A remarkable brand performance isn't just about meeting expectations; it's about exceeding them, consistently and authentically. It's about crafting an experience that resonates with your audience, builds trust, and leaves a lasting impression. In this chapter, we embark on a journey to unravel the intricacies of brand performance and discover how it can be harnessed to propel your brand to new heights.

Customer Journey Mapping: Charting the Path

At the heart of brand performance lies the customer journey, a path woven through a series of interactions between your brand and your audience. But to truly understand this journey, we must first create a map—a blueprint that illuminates the twists and turns, the highs and lows, and the moments that matter most.

Customer journey mapping is the art of visualizing the entire experience that your customers go through when they interact with your brand. It provides a bird's-eye view of their interactions, emotions, and decision-making processes. A well-crafted customer journey map serves as a compass, guiding your brand to create meaningful connections and navigate toward exceptional brand experiences.

Benefits of Customer Journey Mapping

The advantages of customer journey mapping extend far beyond the surface. By embarking on this journey of exploration and understanding, you unlock a plethora of benefits:

Insightful Understanding: Gain a deep understanding of your customers' needs, pain points, and desires, empowering you to tailor your brand's approach to meet their expectations.

Enhanced Customer Experience: Identify opportunities to enhance the customer experience at every touchpoint, making it more seamless, enjoyable, and memorable.

Alignment: Align your brand's efforts, messaging, and resources with the stages of the customer journey, ensuring consistency and relevance.

Problem Solving: Pinpoint bottlenecks, pain points, and hurdles in the customer journey, allowing you to proactively address issues and improve overall satisfaction.

Competitive Advantage: Stand out in a crowded marketplace by delivering experiences that go beyond your competitors' offerings.

Steps to Create a Customer Journey Map

Creating an effective customer journey map involves a systematic approach, drawing upon data, insights, and empathy. Here are the key steps to embark on this enlightening process:

Define Personas: Start by identifying your target audience personas. Understand their demographics, behaviors, goals, and pain points.

Data Collection: Gather data on customer interactions, feedback, and touchpoints. This could include surveys, interviews, website analytics, and social media insights.

Mapping Stages: Break down the customer journey into distinct stages, from awareness and consideration to purchase and post-purchase.

Touchpoint Analysis: For each stage, analyze the touchpoints where customers interact with your brand. This includes your website, social media, customer service, and more.

Customer Emotions: Dive into the emotional journey of your customers. Understand their feelings, motivations, and frustrations at each stage.

Create the Map: Visualize the customer journey map, incorporating the gathered insights, touchpoints, and emotions. Use visuals, such as flowcharts or infographics, to make it accessible and understandable.

Using Customer Journey Maps for Brand Improvement

A customer journey map is not just a static document; it's a dynamic tool for brand enhancement. Once created, your map becomes a strategic resource that informs your decision-making processes, helping you improve your brand's performance. It enables you to:

Identify Pain Points: Uncover areas in the customer journey where customers may face challenges or frustrations, allowing you to address and mitigate these pain points.

Tailor Communication: Craft messages, content, and interactions that resonate with customers at each stage of their journey, enhancing engagement and satisfaction.

Optimize Touchpoints: Continuously refine your touchpoints, such as your website or customer support, to ensure they align with customer expectations.

Measure Success: Use your customer journey map as a benchmark to track improvements and gauge the impact of your brand performance efforts.

Embarking on a journey of customer journey mapping is a transformative step in elevating your brand's performance. By understanding the intricacies of your customers' experiences, you pave the way for delivering exceptional brand interactions and forging lasting connections.

In the subsequent sections of this chapter, we'll explore additional facets of brand performance, diving into the art of customer service, building emotional connections, anticipating needs, and measuring and evaluating your brand's impact. Let's continue this enlightening journey toward brand excellence.

Customer Service Excellence: Elevating the Experience

In the intricate tapestry of brand performance, exceptional customer service stands as a pillar of distinction. It's not merely a transaction; it's a relationship, an opportunity to leave an indelible mark on your customers. Understanding the profound significance of exceptional customer service is paramount.

Exceptional customer service is more than just providing solutions to problems; it's about creating an experience that leaves your customers feeling valued, understood, and delighted. It's a reflection of your brand's commitment to going above and beyond to ensure customer satisfaction.

This dedication to customer service excellence yields manifold benefits:

Loyalty and Retention: Exceptional service fosters customer loyalty, encouraging repeat business and long-term relationships.

Word-of-Mouth Marketing: Satisfied customers become brand advocates, sharing their positive experiences with others and expanding your brand's reach.

Competitive Advantage: Exceptional service differentiates your brand in a crowded marketplace, positioning you as a preferred choice.

Brand Image: Your customer service interactions directly impact your brand's image, shaping perceptions and building trust.

Profitability: Happy customers are more likely to spend more, increasing your brand's profitability.

Strategies for Providing Outstanding Customer Service

Achieving exceptional customer service isn't a mere aspiration; it's a strategic endeavor. Here are some key strategies to infuse your brand's customer service with excellence:

Training and Empowerment: Your customer service team serves as the frontline ambassadors of your brand. Invest in their training to ensure they not only understand but also embody your brand's values, mission, and persona. Empower them with the authority to make decisions that enhance the customer experience, fostering a sense of ownership.

Responsive Communication: Timeliness is of the essence in customer service. Ensure that customer inquiries, concerns, and feedback receive prompt and effective responses. A swift resolution of issues not only resolves problems but also demonstrates a genuine commitment to customer satisfaction.

Consistency: Consistency is the bedrock of exceptional service. Maintain a uniform level of service quality across all customer service channels, whether it's in-person, over the phone, or online. Customers should experience the same level of care and attentiveness regardless of the communication medium.

Personalization: Customers appreciate being treated as individuals, not numbers. Personalize interactions by addressing customers by name and acknowledging their history with your brand. Leverage data and insights to tailor recommendations and solutions to their specific needs and preferences.

Handling Customer Complaints and Feedback

In the realm of customer service excellence, how you handle complaints and feedback can make all the difference. These moments of friction are opportunities to transform dissatisfied customers into loyal advocates. Here's how to navigate them effectively:

Active Listening: When a customer voices a concern, listen attentively without interruption. Allow them to express their feelings and concerns fully.

Empathy: Empathize with the customer's perspective and emotions. Acknowledge their feelings and demonstrate understanding.

Swift Action: Act promptly to address the issue. Ensure that the customer knows you are taking their concern seriously.

Resolution: Strive for a resolution that exceeds the customer's expectations. Go the extra mile to rectify the situation and ensure their satisfaction.

Feedback Integration: Use customer feedback as a valuable resource for improvement. Continuously assess your processes and procedures to prevent similar issues in the future.

Training Your Team for Exceptional Service

To achieve exceptional customer service consistently, investing in the training and development of your customer service team is imperative. Here are key steps to ensure your team is well-prepared:

Onboarding and Orientation: Start by providing comprehensive onboarding and orientation programs to familiarize new team members with your brand's culture, values, and customer service philosophy.

Ongoing Training: Customer service training should be an ongoing process. Regularly update your team on new products, services, and procedures, as well as evolving customer expectations.

Role Play: Conduct role-playing exercises to simulate real customer interactions. This helps team members practice effective communication and problem-solving.

Feedback and Assessment: Provide constructive feedback and performance assessments to identify areas for improvement and recognize outstanding service.

Empowerment: Empower your team with the authority to make decisions that benefit the customer, minimizing the need for escalation.

Exceptional customer service isn't a one-time achievement; it's a commitment that must be woven into the fabric of your brand. By understanding its significance, implementing key strategies, and empowering your team, you can elevate the customer experience and set the stage for exceptional brand performance.

Building Emotional Connections: Beyond Transactions

Emotions are the currency of human connections, and in the world of branding, emotional connections wield immense power. Building emotional connections with your audience transcends mere transactions; it forges lasting relationships with your brand at the core. Understanding the potency of emotional branding is pivotal.

Emotionally connected customers are not just loyal; they are advocates, passionate about your brand and eager to share their experiences. They are more forgiving of occasional missteps and are willing to pay a premium for the value your brand provides. Emotional branding transforms customers into an integral part of your brand story.

This section explores the significance of emotional branding, delves into techniques for eliciting emotions in branding, provides illuminating case studies of brands that excel in this domain, and discusses how to measure the strength of emotional connections.

Techniques for Eliciting Emotions in Branding

Eliciting emotions in branding is a craft that requires finesse. It's about creating an authentic and resonant narrative that touches the hearts and minds of your audience. Here are some techniques to master this art:

Storytelling: Craft compelling brand stories that evoke emotions, painting a vivid picture of your brand's journey, values, and impact on the world.

Visual Imagery: Leverage imagery and design elements that resonate with your brand's emotional tone. Colors, fonts, and imagery can evoke specific emotions.

Personalization: Tailor your messaging and offerings to individual customer preferences, making them feel valued and understood.

Brand Voice: Develop a brand voice that embodies the emotions you wish to convey. Is your brand caring, humorous, or inspirational? Your tone should align with your chosen emotions.

User Experience: Create seamless and delightful user experiences that leave a positive emotional imprint on your customers.

Case Studies: Brands that Excel in Emotional Branding

To truly grasp the power of emotional branding, we'll explore case studies of brands that have mastered this art. These brands have created emotional connections that endure and continue to resonate with their audiences.

Apple: Apple's brand is built on emotions like innovation, creativity, and simplicity. Their iconic product launches, with Steve Jobs as the charismatic presenter, created excitement and emotional connections among their customers.

Coca-Cola: Coca-Cola is known for its heartwarming and inclusive marketing campaigns, such as the "Share a Coke" initiative. These campaigns evoke emotions of happiness and togetherness.

Nike: Nike's "Just Do It" slogan and powerful advertisements inspire emotions like determination and courage, resonating with athletes and anyone striving to overcome challenges.

Measuring Emotional Connection

While the emotional connection between your brand and customers may seem intangible, it can be quantified and assessed. Understanding the strength of this connection is essential for refining your emotional branding strategies. Here are some methods and metrics for measuring emotional connection:

Surveys and Feedback: Collect customer feedback and conduct surveys to gauge their emotional responses to your brand. Ask questions that uncover emotional sentiments.

Social Media Monitoring: Analyze social media conversations and mentions of your brand to understand the emotional tone of customer interactions.

Net Promoter Score (NPS): NPS surveys can reveal the emotional attachment customers have to your brand by asking if they would recommend it to others.

Customer Loyalty and Advocacy: Track metrics related to customer loyalty, such as repeat purchases and referrals, as emotionally connected customers are more likely to become brand advocates.

Qualitative Analysis: Dive deep into qualitative data, including customer reviews and testimonials, to uncover emotional themes and sentiments.

By measuring emotional connection, you can gain insights into how well your brand resonates with your audience emotionally and make informed decisions to strengthen these connections further. Emotional branding isn't just about making customers feel; it's about making them feel a certain way that aligns with your brand's values and personality.

The Art of Anticipatory Customer Service

Anticipatory customer service is a proactive approach to meeting customer needs before they even articulate them. It's about surpassing expectations by intuitively understanding what your customers want. The art of anticipatory customer service can set your brand apart.

Customers appreciate when their needs are anticipated, as it demonstrates a deep understanding and commitment to their satisfaction. This section explores the art of anticipatory customer service, offering insights into how to excel in this domain.

Predictive Analytics in Branding

Predictive analytics is a powerful tool for anticipating customer needs. By analyzing data and trends, you can make informed predictions about customer behavior and preferences. We'll explore how predictive analytics can be harnessed for branding, enabling you to stay one step ahead of your customers' needs.

Personalization and Customization

Personalization is the act of tailoring products, services, and experiences to individual customer preferences. It's about making each customer feel like your brand was designed just for them. In this section, we'll delve into the art of personalization and customization, discussing strategies to implement these approaches effectively.

The Role of Artificial Intelligence

Artificial intelligence (AI) is revolutionizing how brands anticipate and meet customer needs. AI-powered chatbots, recommendation engines, and data analysis tools can provide personalized experiences at scale. We'll explore the role of AI in anticipatory customer service and how it can elevate your brand's performance.

By mastering the art of emotional branding, anticipatory customer service, and leveraging technologies like predictive analytics and AI, your brand can not only meet but exceed customer expectations. Building emotional connections and anticipating needs are integral components of exceptional brand performance, creating a customer-centric approach that fosters loyalty and advocacy.

Marketing Channels and Touch Points

In the dynamic landscape of brand performance, marketing channels and touchpoints are the conduits through which your brand message flows to reach your audience. The effectiveness of these channels can significantly influence how your brand is perceived, the relationships you build with your customers, and the overall impact you have on your market.

This section delves into the strategic aspects of brand performance within the digital realm. It explores how product and service design can elevate customer experiences, why your website is the cornerstone of your online presence, and how to harness the power of social media to engage your audience effectively. By understanding and optimizing these vital elements, you can create a brand presence that not only captivates but also leaves a lasting impression, driving meaningful connections and fostering brand loyalty.

Designing Products and Services for Exceptional Experiences

Exceptional brand performance isn't solely about what you say; it's about what you do. This includes designing products and services that go beyond meeting customer needs – they exceed expectations, create memorable experiences, and align with your brand's values.

Here's why focusing on user experience, innovation, and customer satisfaction in product and service design is essential:

User-Centered Design: Start with your customers in mind. Understand their pain points, preferences, and aspirations. User-centered design ensures that your products and services cater to their needs.

Innovation: Innovation keeps your brand relevant and competitive. Encourage a culture of innovation that allows you to stay ahead of the curve and provide cutting-edge solutions.

Customer Satisfaction: Satisfied customers are more likely to become loyal advocates for your brand. Exceptional products and services lead to higher levels of satisfaction.

Continuous Improvement: Use customer feedback and data to iterate and improve your offerings continually. A commitment to improvement shows that your brand values its customers' input.

This section explores how effective product and service design can enhance brand performance, drive customer loyalty, and establish a reputation for excellence.

The Role of Your Website in Brand Performance

In today's digital age, your website serves as the digital face of your brand. It's often the first touchpoint customers encounter, making its role in brand performance critical. Your website is more than an online brochure; it's a dynamic platform for building trust, delivering value, and facilitating meaningful interactions. Here's why your website is indispensable:

Building Trust: A well-designed website instills trust and credibility. Customers are more likely to engage with a brand they trust, increasing the chances of conversion.

Delivering Value: Your website should provide value to visitors. This can be through informative content, resources, tools, or e-commerce capabilities. A valuable website keeps visitors engaged and encourages return visits.

Central Hub: Your website serves as the central hub for your online presence. It connects your various online touchpoints, such as social media, email marketing, and e-commerce. A cohesive online presence reinforces your brand identity.

User Experience: A seamless and user-friendly website enhances the overall user experience. Easy navigation, fast load times, and responsive design are crucial factors in retaining visitors.

This section explores the critical role your website plays in brand performance, offers insights into optimizing your website for maximum impact, and highlights the importance of a user-focused approach.

Leveraging Social Media for Brand Engagement

Social media platforms have transformed the way brands engage with their audiences. They offer dynamic opportunities for building a community, amplifying brand messages, and fostering meaningful interactions. Effective social media usage can significantly enhance brand performance. Here's why:

Audience Engagement: Social media platforms provide direct channels to engage with your audience, listen to their feedback, and respond to their inquiries. Authentic engagement builds relationships.

Community Building: Brands can create communities of loyal followers who share common interests and values. These communities become advocates and brand ambassadors.

Amplification: Social media amplifies your brand's reach. Engaging content can go viral, increasing brand visibility and attracting new audiences.

Content Sharing: Social media platforms facilitate content sharing. Brands can share valuable content, including blog posts, videos, infographics, and more, to educate and entertain their audience.

Additional Touchpoints

In the digital age, where online interactions often take center stage, it's easy to overlook the importance of traditional touchpoints and physical spaces. Yet, these tangible elements of your brand presence wield immense power in shaping brand perception and creating memorable experiences.

Packaging: Delve into the significance of packaging design and its role in influencing the overall brand experience. Learn how thoughtful packaging can turn routine unboxing moments into exciting adventures and enhance your brand's in-store appeal. Discover the art of using packaging as a tool for storytelling and emotional connection.

Business Collateral: Explore the world of business collateral, including brochures, business cards, and promotional materials. These tangible assets contribute to brand consistency and professionalism. Learn how to design and utilize business collateral effectively to leave a lasting impression on your clients and partners.

Physical Spaces: Physical spaces, whether retail stores, offices, or event venues, have a substantial impact on brand perception. Dive into the strategies for creating spaces that reflect your brand's identity and values. Understand how the layout, decor, and ambiance of your physical spaces can influence customer experiences and strengthen brand loyalty.

Apps: Branded mobile applications are powerful tools for enhancing customer engagement and streamlining processes. Explore the world of app design and development. Discover how a well-designed app can offer unique value to your customers and create a seamless and enjoyable brand experience.

Podcasts and Webinars: Podcasts and webinars have emerged as dynamic platforms for brand storytelling, thought leadership, and audience education. Learn how to leverage these audio and video formats to connect with your audience on a deeper level. Explore strategies for creating engaging and informative content that aligns with your brand's messaging and values.

In this section, we uncover the potential of these additional touchpoints to reinforce your brand identity and elevate the overall brand experience. By harnessing the power of both traditional and digital touchpoints, you can create a well-rounded and unforgettable brand presence that resonates with your audience and stands out in the crowded marketplace.

Measuring and Evaluating Performance: The Metrics of Success

Brand performance isn't just about implementing strategies; it's about knowing how well those strategies are working and making data-driven improvements. In this final section, we delve into the critical aspect of measuring and evaluating your brand's performance.

Performance Metrics: Explore the world of key performance indicators (KPIs) and metrics that businesses can leverage to assess the effectiveness of their brand performance strategies. Learn how to identify the right KPIs for your brand, measure brand awareness, track customer engagement, and monitor other vital factors that contribute to your brand's success.

To ensure your brand performance aligns with your brand's purpose, persona, and personality, employ key performance indicators (KPIs) and metrics:

Customer Satisfaction (CSAT): Measure overall customer satisfaction through post-interaction surveys.

Net Promoter Score (NPS): Determine customer loyalty and the likelihood of recommending your brand to others.

Customer Effort Score (CES): Assess the ease with which customers can achieve their goals when interacting with your brand.

Customer Retention Rate: Track the percentage of customers who continue to engage with your brand over time.

Response and Resolution Times: Monitor the speed and efficiency of customer service interactions.

Data Analysis: In the age of data, understanding customer behavior and identifying trends is paramount. Discover the importance of data analysis in evaluating brand performance. Uncover how data-driven insights can inform your decisions, refine your strategies, and drive continuous improvement.

Feedback and Surveys: Your customers hold valuable insights into your brand's performance. Learn why gathering feedback from customers and conducting surveys is a strategic imperative. Discover how these tools can provide a deeper understanding of customer satisfaction, loyalty, and areas for improvement.

Creating Your Own Case Study: Case studies offer tangible proof of effective brand performance strategies in action. Learn how to create your own case study to measure and evaluate your brand's work. Gain valuable insights into how these brands achieved their goals and the impact of their strategies on their market presence and bottom line.

In this section, we close the loop on the brand performance journey, emphasizing the importance of continuous improvement and data-driven decision-making. Armed with the knowledge and tools to measure and evaluate your brand's performance, you can steer your brand toward greater success, ensuring that it remains relevant, resonates with your audience, and continues to thrive in a dynamic marketplace.

CHAPTER 09
**CULTIVATING YOUR
PERSONAL BRAND**

I n our journey through the realms of branding, we've explored the intricate tapestry of crafting brands that matter. We've delved into the depths of brand purpose, persona, personality, proclamation, positioning, presence, and performance. We've uncovered the secrets of creating a brand that resonates, engages, and thrives in a competitive landscape. Now, in the final chapter of our brand alchemy adventure, we turn the spotlight on a pivotal aspect that holds immense potential for all careers: Personal Branding.

The Essence of Personal Branding

Personal branding is more than a buzzword; it's the art of packaging and presenting yourself to the world in a way that leaves a lasting impression. Just as we've woven intricate brand stories and positioned businesses, your personal brand is a narrative that defines who you are, what you stand for, and what you bring to the table.

While personal branding is often associated with entrepreneurs, influencers, and public figures, it's a valuable asset for individuals across all career paths. Whether you're a corporate professional, a creative artist, a scientist, or an educator, personal branding empowers you to shape how you're perceived, connect with your audience, and advance your career.

The Power of Personal Branding

1. Career Advancement

In today's dynamic job market, personal branding is your passport to career advancement. It helps you stand out from the crowd and positions you as an authority in your field. When you have a strong personal brand, employers and peers recognize your expertise, trust your judgment, and are more likely to consider you for leadership roles and promotions.

2. Building Influence

Your personal brand is your platform for sharing your knowledge, ideas, and passions with a broader audience. By establishing yourself as a thought leader, you can influence industry trends, drive change, and inspire others in your field. Personal branding allows you to become a recognized voice, making you a go-to expert for insights and opinions.

3. Networking and Partnerships

A well-crafted personal brand opens doors to meaningful connections and collaborations. It attracts like-minded individuals who share your values and aspirations. Whether you're seeking partnerships, mentorship, or collaboration opportunities, a strong personal brand makes you an attractive proposition for potential collaborators and allies.

4. Confidence and Self-Expression

Personal branding isn't just about how others perceive you; it's also a journey of self-discovery and self-expression. It encourages you to define your values, strengths, and unique qualities. This self-awareness boosts your confidence, enabling you to navigate challenges, take risks, and seize opportunities with conviction.

5. Adaptability

In an evolving professional landscape, personal branding equips you with the adaptability needed to thrive in different career phases. Your brand can evolve as you grow, allowing you to pivot, explore new ventures, and stay relevant in changing industries.

6. Brand Alignment

Personal branding aligns your professional journey with your personal values and passions. When your career reflects your true self, you're more likely to find fulfillment, purpose, and long-term satisfaction.

Crafting Your Personal Brand

In the digital age, personal branding has evolved from a concept into a necessity. It's not just for celebrities or influencers; it's a powerful tool for professionals in every field. Just as we've delved into the building blocks of successful brand identities – purpose, persona, and personality – your personal brand encompasses unique and interconnected facets.

Your personal brand is the sum of who you are and what you stand for in the professional realm. It's not just about self-promotion; it's about establishing a genuine connection with your audience, conveying your values and expertise, and leaving a lasting impression. Your personal brand is the compass that guides your career choices, influences how others perceive you, and ultimately defines your impact.

This section is dedicated to exploring the essential components that make up your personal brand. From understanding your core identity to shaping your voice and resonating with your desired audience, we'll navigate the intricacies of crafting a personal brand that is not only authentic but also instrumental in achieving your professional aspirations. Through thoughtful introspection and strategic positioning, you'll discover how to cultivate a personal brand that is as unique and impactful as you are.

Identity: Who You Are at Your Core?

Your identity is the foundation of your personal brand. It's a deep reflection of your true self, encompassing your core values, beliefs, and experiences. Consider your upbringing, life experiences, and the moments that have shaped you. Your identity should resonate with authenticity and honesty. It's the unchanging essence that defines you and forms the bedrock of your personal brand.

Values: The Principles That Guide Your Decisions

Your values are the compass that guides your personal and professional choices. They represent the principles you hold dear, shaping your behavior and decision-making. To define your personal brand's values, reflect on what matters most to you. How do you approach ethical dilemmas, and what causes or issues are close to your heart? Your values will drive your actions and resonate with those who share similar principles.

Voice: Your Unique Perspective and Communication Style

Your voice in personal branding is how you express yourself authentically. It's your unique perspective, communication style, and tone. Your voice should be consistent across all your brand touchpoints, whether it's in written content, speeches, or social media interactions. Consider how you want your audience to perceive you – as approachable, authoritative, friendly, or motivational. Your voice should align with your brand persona, fostering connection and relatability.

Expertise: Your Knowledge and Skills in Your Domain

Expertise is the domain where you excel and showcase your authority. It's your depth of knowledge, skills, and the value you bring to your audience. Your expertise is closely tied to your brand persona and values. It's what sets you apart and positions you as a credible source. Identify your unique skills and experiences that position you as an expert in your field, and emphasize them in your personal branding.

Passions: What Fuels Your Creativity and Drive

Your passions are the driving force behind your personal brand. They're the interests and pursuits that ignite your creativity and enthusiasm. When crafting your personal brand, consider how your passions align with your values and expertise. Your passions add depth and authenticity to your brand story, making it more relatable and engaging. Sharing your passions can also attract like-minded individuals who resonate with your interests.

Audience: The People You Want to Connect With

Your audience is at the heart of your personal brand. To craft a successful personal brand, you must define and understand your target audience. Who are the individuals you want to connect with, inspire, or influence? Create detailed audience personas, considering demographics, psychographics, and behaviors. Tailor your personal brand message to resonate with your intended audience, building meaningful connections.

Presence: How You Show Up in Various Contexts

Your presence encompasses how you present yourself in different situations and environments. It's about being adaptable and mindful of context while remaining true to your personal brand's core identity and values. Your presence should be consistent, whether you're networking, giving a presentation, or engaging on social media. It's the art of showing up authentically and purposefully in a way that aligns with your personal brand.

By diving deeper into these facets of your personal brand, you'll have a solid foundation for crafting a compelling and authentic personal brand identity. Consider how each facet intertwines with your brand purpose, persona, and personality, creating a harmonious and impactful personal brand that resonates with your target audience.

Your Personal Branding Journey

Embarking on a personal branding journey involves self-reflection, strategic planning, and consistent effort. It's about curating an authentic online presence, sharing your insights through content creation, and engaging with your audience. Whether it's through social media, blogging, public speaking, or networking, your personal brand comes alive through every interaction.

As you venture into the world of personal branding, remember that it's an ongoing process of refinement and growth. Be open to feedback, stay true to your values, and keep evolving your brand to align with your aspirations.

Your personal brand is a dynamic force that can elevate your career, amplify your influence, and enrich your life. It's not just about leaving a mark on the world but making a meaningful impact on the people you connect with.

In the ever-changing landscape of work and careers, your personal brand is your anchor, your guiding star, and your compass. It's your unique legacy in the world of brand alchemy.

So, as we conclude our exploration of branding's diverse dimensions, remember that your personal brand is an invaluable asset that can shape your path, fulfill your dreams, and leave an indelible mark on the world. It's time to embark on your personal branding journey and unlock the boundless potential within you.

CHAPTER 10
HOW TO USE DESIGN THINKING
TO CREATE YOUR BRAND

In today's competitive business landscape, crafting a brand that merely captivates is no longer enough. To truly thrive, your brand must form deep and lasting connections with your target audience. In this chapter, we embark on a journey through the principles of design thinking to unveil a step-by-step process that prioritizes human needs, emotions, and experiences at the very heart of brand creation.

Design thinking is not merely a methodology; it's a mindset that champions empathy, creativity, and innovation. It challenges the conventional and propels brands to break free from the shackles of mediocrity. The core tenets of design thinking—empathizing with your audience, defining their pain points, ideating innovative solutions, prototyping, and testing—empower brands to go beyond aesthetics and surface-level interactions. Instead, they can delve deep into the psyche of their audience, forming connections that resonate on profound levels.

Our journey through this chapter will be an exploration of the transformative power of design thinking. We will guide you through the process, from understanding your audience's unique challenges and desires to creating meaningful solutions that resonate with their core values. Along the way, we will provide practical insights, actionable strategies, and real-world examples to illustrate the immense potential of design thinking in crafting brands that not only stand out but also leave a lasting imprint in the hearts and minds of your audience.

So, let's dive in and discover how design thinking can be your compass on this exciting journey towards crafting a brand that doesn't just captivate but fosters authentic connections that endure and flourish.

Step 1: Empathize with Your Audience

In the world of brand creation, empathy forms the bedrock of deep and enduring connections with your audience. It's not merely about knowing your customers; it's about understanding them on an emotional level, tapping into their desires, and addressing their most profound pain points. This empathetic approach lays the foundation for a brand that resonates authentically with its audience.

In our exploration of this critical stage, we'll draw upon key learnings and insights from the earlier chapter on "Know Your Audience." Here, we expand upon those principles, offering concrete strategies, tools, and methodologies to help you truly empathize with your audience.

Surveys, Interviews, and Data Analytics: To embark on the path of empathy, you'll want to utilize a combination of research methods. Surveys and interviews allow you to engage directly with your audience, delving into their thoughts, emotions, and experiences. The insights gained from these personal interactions are invaluable, as they provide qualitative data that can uncover hidden motivations and sentiments.

On the other hand, data analytics offers a quantitative perspective. By analyzing data related to customer behavior, preferences, and engagement, you can identify patterns and trends that offer a deeper understanding of your audience's needs.

Creating Empathy Maps: An empathy map is a powerful tool that helps you visualize the emotional landscape of your audience. It prompts you to consider what your audience thinks, feels, says, and does, providing a holistic view of their experiences. Empathy maps serve as valuable reference points throughout your brand creation journey, ensuring you remain aligned with your audience's emotional state.

Persona Development: Crafting detailed audience personas based on your research findings enables you to personify the individuals you aim to connect with. These personas should encompass not only demographic data but also the emotional dimensions of your audience. What are their fears, aspirations, and motivations? What challenges do they face? By humanizing your audience in this way, you can better empathize with their unique situations.

Storytelling as a Tool: The power of storytelling is undeniable. To truly empathize with your audience, consider creating narratives that mirror their experiences and emotions. Stories have an innate ability to evoke empathy by allowing your audience to step into the shoes of the characters. This approach fosters a deeper connection and understanding between your brand and your audience.

In summary, empathizing with your audience is not a one-time effort but an ongoing commitment. By employing the strategies, tools, and methodologies outlined in this section, you'll not only gain insights into your audience's deepest desires and pain points but also create a brand that resonates on a profound emotional level.

Step 2: Define Your Brand Purpose

With a profound understanding of your audience, it's time to embark on a journey to define your brand's raison d'être. This step is not just about crafting a mission statement; it's about uncovering the core essence of your brand—the "why" that fuels your existence. Your brand's purpose is more than just a statement; it's the North Star that guides every branding decision you make.

Key Learnings from the Chapter on Purpose:

In the chapter dedicated to defining your brand's purpose, we explored the art of discovering the profound reason behind your brand's existence. Here are some key learnings and insights that you can carry forward into this step:

The Power of Why: We discussed how brands with a clear and compelling "why" resonate deeply with their audience. They inspire not only loyalty but also advocacy. This chapter emphasized the importance of having a purpose that transcends profit.

Aligning Values: We touched upon the significance of aligning your brand's values with those of your audience. When your values resonate with your customers, it fosters a sense of belonging and shared purpose.

Tools for Discovery: We introduced various tools and exercises to help you uncover your brand's purpose. This included exploring your personal values, conducting customer surveys, and analyzing competitor landscapes.

Now, with these key learnings in mind, it's time to define your brand's purpose with clarity and conviction. Here's how to proceed:

Crafting Your Brand's Purpose:

The Change You Wish to Manifest: Reflect on the change you aspire to bring to the world. What societal or personal transformation does your brand seek to achieve? This could involve addressing a pressing issue, simplifying a complex process, or enhancing the quality of life for your audience.

Values That Guide Your Journey: Recall the values that emerged from your explorations in the chapter on defining your brand's purpose. These values should serve as the foundation upon which your purpose is built. They are the principles that define how your brand behaves and interacts with the world.

Clarity and Conviction: Write your brand's purpose statement with clarity and conviction. It should be concise yet powerful, capturing the essence of what you stand for and the impact you aim to make. Your purpose statement should resonate with both your team and your audience.

Alignment with Audience Needs: Ensure that your brand's purpose aligns with the needs, desires, and aspirations of your target audience. It should resonate with them on a profound level, igniting a sense of connection and shared purpose.

Integration into Branding Decisions: Keep your brand's purpose at the forefront of all branding decisions. Whether you're designing a logo, crafting a marketing campaign, or making a strategic business move, your purpose should serve as the compass that guides you.

In this step, your mission is to define your brand's purpose with such clarity and conviction that it becomes the driving force behind every action you take. Your purpose should not only be a statement on paper but a living, breathing force that shapes your brand's identity and impact on the world.

Step 3: Ideate and Innovate

In this phase of brand development, you enter the creative realm where the magic of branding truly comes to life. You'll generate a multitude of ideas and concepts to shape every aspect of your brand, aligning them with your brand's core purpose. This process is essential for developing a unique, memorable, and impactful brand identity.

Brainstorming Sessions

Brainstorming sessions are a classic and effective way to ignite creativity within your team or collaborative group. The aim is to encourage open and unfiltered idea generation, allowing all participants to contribute without fear of judgment. Here's how to make the most of brainstorming sessions:

1. Preparation: Define the specific branding pillar or aspect you want to brainstorm about. It could be anything from brand personality traits to ideas for your brand proclamation.

2. Select Participants: Gather a diverse group of individuals with varying perspectives. The richness of ideas often comes from different viewpoints.

3. Set Clear Goals: Clearly communicate the objectives of the brainstorming session. What do you want to achieve? What problem are you trying to solve or what ideas are you seeking?

4. Encourage Free Thinking: Create a non-judgmental and welcoming environment where participants feel comfortable expressing even the wildest ideas. Encourage quantity over quality at this stage.

5. Use Facilitation Techniques: Employ facilitation techniques like "round-robin" or "brainwriting," where each participant contributes ideas one by one. This ensures everyone's voice is heard.

6. Capture Ideas: Record all ideas, whether on a whiteboard, sticky notes, or a digital platform. Visualizing the ideas can help spark further creativity.

7. Build on Ideas: Encourage participants to build on each other's ideas. Often, one idea can trigger another, leading to innovative concepts.

8. Time Constraints: Set a time limit for the brainstorming session to maintain focus and energy. However, don't rush the process; ensure there's ample time for idea generation.

9. Review and Select: Once the session is complete, review the ideas and select the most promising ones for further development.

Mind Mapping

Mind mapping is a powerful visual tool for organizing and connecting ideas. It helps you explore the relationships between different aspects of your brand and discover new opportunities. Here's how to utilize mind mapping effectively:

1. Start with the Core Idea: Begin with your brand's core purpose or a specific pillar you're brainstorming about.

2. Create Branches: Branch out from the core idea with related concepts or subtopics. For example, if you're mind-mapping brand personality, you might create branches for traits like "innovative," "friendly," or "adventurous."

3. Connect and Expand: Use lines or arrows to connect related ideas. As you expand your mind map, you'll uncover connections and patterns that can lead to innovative branding concepts.

4. Visualize Relationships: The visual nature of mind maps helps you see the relationships between ideas, making it easier to identify strengths, weaknesses, opportunities, and threats.

SWOT Analysis

A SWOT analysis is a structured approach to evaluating your brand's strengths, weaknesses, opportunities, and threats. It provides a comprehensive view of your brand's current position and can inform your ideation process effectively:

Strengths: Identify and leverage your brand's internal strengths, such as unique expertise, exceptional customer service, or a strong online presence. These strengths can be built upon and used as differentiators.

Weaknesses: Acknowledge areas where your brand may be lacking, whether it's in customer service, product quality, or market reach. Identifying weaknesses allows you to address them in your branding strategy.

Opportunities: Explore external opportunities that your brand can capitalize on. These could include market trends, emerging technologies, or unmet customer needs. Opportunities are fertile ground for innovative ideas.

Threats: Recognize external threats that could negatively impact your brand, such as changing market conditions, competition, or economic factors. Identifying threats enables you to develop strategies to mitigate risks.

By conducting a SWOT analysis for each branding pillar, you gain a deeper understanding of your brand's current standing and uncover areas where innovation and improvement are needed.

Remember, the ideation phase is a dynamic and creative process. Embrace these techniques to unleash your brand's full potential and develop innovative concepts that resonate with your audience and align with your brand's core purpose.

Step 4: Prototype Your Brand

With your innovative ideas generated and your brand pillars defined, it's time to bring your brand to life through tangible prototypes. This phase involves sketching, crafting, and designing various elements that collectively form your brand identity. By creating prototypes, you not only visualize your brand in its early stages but also open the door to further refinement.

Sketch Logo Concepts

Logo design is one of the most critical aspects of your brand identity. Begin by sketching out various logo concepts based on your brand's purpose, personality, and positioning. These sketches don't need to be polished; they're meant to capture the essence of your brand visually.

Craft Compelling Taglines

Taglines are memorable phrases that encapsulate your brand's essence or value proposition. Craft multiple tagline options that align with your brand's core purpose and persona. These taglines should be concise, clear, and emotionally resonant with your audience.

Design Visual Elements

Visual elements play a pivotal role in brand identity. Design your color palettes and typography choices to create a cohesive and harmonious visual identity. Consider the emotions and associations these visual elements evoke and ensure they align with your brand's values and messaging.

Create Prototypes

With your logo sketches, tagline options, and visual elements in hand, create prototypes of your brand's identity. These prototypes can be digital or physical representations that provide a tangible sense of your brand's look and feel. For example, you might create digital mock-ups of how your logo and color palette would appear on a website or physical prototypes of packaging designs.

Visualize Your Brand

The prototyping phase allows you to visualize your brand's early identity and see how its various elements come together cohesively. It's an opportunity to explore different combinations and configurations, ensuring they align with your brand's core purpose and resonate with your target audience.

Prototyping is a creative process that transforms abstract ideas into a tangible brand identity, setting the stage for the next steps in refining and finalizing your brand.

Step 5: Test and Gather Feedback

With your brand prototypes in hand, it's time to put them to the test with your target audience. This phase involves seeking feedback and gathering insights that will help you refine and perfect your brand identity. Here's how to effectively test and refine your brand:

Engage Focus Groups

Organize focus groups consisting of individuals from your target audience. This provides you with a direct line to potential customers who can offer valuable feedback on your brand elements. Ask them about their perceptions, emotions, and associations with your brand prototypes.

Leverage Surveys

Create surveys that are distributed to a broader audience, including both potential and existing customers. Surveys are a scalable way to collect opinions and preferences regarding your brand's logo concepts, taglines, color palettes, and other visual elements. Make sure your survey questions are well-crafted to extract actionable insights.

Implement Beta Testing

If applicable, conduct beta testing of your brand elements. For instance, if you're developing a new website, release a beta version to a select group of users. Their real-world interactions will reveal usability issues and other areas for improvement. Beta testing is particularly useful for digital products and services.

Listen to Feedback

Pay close attention to the feedback you receive during focus group sessions, through surveys, and from beta testing. Analyze common themes and trends in the feedback. Some elements may resonate positively, while others might need adjustments.

Stay Open to Adjustments

Be receptive to making adjustments based on the feedback you receive. If certain aspects of your brand prototypes aren't connecting with your audience as intended, consider making changes. The goal is to ensure that your brand identity aligns with the perceptions and preferences of your target audience.

Testing and refining your brand prototypes is a crucial step in the branding process. It allows you to fine-tune your brand identity to resonate more effectively with your audience and create a lasting impact. Remember that brand development is an iterative process, and the insights you gain during this phase will contribute to the ultimate success of your brand.

Step 6: Implement Your Brand

Having refined your brand identity, it's time to put it into action through comprehensive implementation. This phase involves rolling out your brand across all touchpoints, ensuring a consistent and memorable experience for your audience. Here's how to effectively implement your brand:

1. Consistency Across Touchpoints

Maintain a consistent brand presence across all touchpoints. Whether it's your website, social media profiles, marketing materials, or in-person interactions, your brand should deliver a uniform experience. Consistency fosters trust and recognition among your audience.

2. Website Integration

Your website is often the central hub of your brand's online presence. Ensure that your brand identity is seamlessly integrated into your website design, including logos, color palettes, typography, and messaging. Visitors should immediately recognize your brand when they land on your site.

3. Social Media Cohesion

Leverage social media platforms to amplify your brand message. Consistency is key here as well. Maintain uniform branding elements across your social profiles, such as profile pictures, cover photos, and content style. Engage with your audience authentically to build a community around your brand.

4. Marketing Materials

Apply your brand identity to all marketing collateral, including brochures, business cards, flyers, and digital advertisements. Ensure that your visual elements, such as logos and color palettes, remain consistent to reinforce brand recognition.

5. Customer Interactions

Train your customer service team to embody your brand's values and persona in every interaction. Whether it's in-person, over the phone, or through digital channels, customer interactions should align with your brand's mission and personality.

6. Physical Spaces

If your brand has physical locations, such as retail stores or offices, incorporate your brand identity into the physical environment. From interior design to signage, create a cohesive and immersive brand experience.

7. Digital Touchpoints

Beyond your website and social media, consider other digital touchpoints like mobile apps, email marketing, and podcasts/

webinars. Apply your brand identity consistently to these channels, maintaining a unified brand voice and style.

Step 7: Iterate and Evolve

Design thinking is a dynamic, iterative process. As your brand takes root, it should evolve in tandem with your audience's ever-changing needs and preferences. Continuously collecting feedback, analyzing data, and remaining adaptable are essential to making the necessary adjustments. Your brand is a living entity, and it must grow and evolve to remain relevant and impactful.

The Power of Continuous Improvement

Building and maintaining a brand with design thinking is not a one-time endeavor but a perpetual journey. It's an ongoing commitment to excellence and innovation. As you follow the meticulously curated steps outlined in this chapter, you'll create a brand that authentically reflects your values and vision while profoundly resonating with your audience.

Staying Aligned with Your Audience

Your audience is not static, and neither should your brand be. The world around us evolves, and your brand must be agile enough to adapt to these changes. By embracing a design thinking approach, you can keep your brand closely aligned with the people it serves.

Fostering Lasting Connections

A brand crafted through design thinking becomes a catalyst for positive change. It establishes lasting connections and drives meaningful impact. It is not just a logo or a tagline but a reflection of your purpose, values, and commitment to your audience.

Conclusion

As you embark on the journey of crafting your brand with design thinking, remember that it's not just about creating a brand; it's about creating a brand experience. This experience should be authentic, compelling, and impactful.

By applying the principles of design thinking, you will be well-equipped to navigate the complexities of modern branding. Your brand will stand out, resonate deeply, and, most importantly, drive positive change in the lives of those it touches.

So, let this chapter serve as your guide, your toolkit, and your source of inspiration as you embark on the transformative journey of building a brand that makes a difference.

CHAPTER 11
ELEVATING YOUR BRAND
BEYOND THE ORDINARY
TO THE EXTRAORDINARY

Branding is not just a superficial layer of business; it's the very essence that defines your success. However, for those who are driven by creativity, conscious entrepreneurship, and the pursuit of meaningful impact, branding takes on an entirely new dimension. It becomes a tool for transformation, a vessel for making a difference, and a guiding light for purpose.

In this concluding chapter, we embark on a journey that transcends the ordinary and dives deep into the heart of branding. We explore the intricacies of this art and science, weaving together the seven pillars that form the very DNA of your brand: purpose, persona, personality, proclamation, positioning, presence, and performance.

But we won't stop at understanding these pillars; we'll elevate them to new heights. This chapter is your guide to infusing creativity and innovation into every aspect of your brand, turning it into a force that leaves an indelible mark on the world. It's a call to action, an invitation to rise above the status quo, and a reminder that your brand can be a catalyst for change and a beacon of inspiration.

Purpose: Igniting Purpose-Driven Innovation

Your brand's purpose is the heartbeat of its existence, the driving force behind its every endeavor. But in the realm of innovation, purpose transcends a static mission statement. It becomes a catalyst for creative problem-solving, dynamic evolution, and impactful change.

Tips for Purpose-Driven Innovation:

Challenge the Status Quo: Revisit your brand's purpose regularly. Encourage your team to question assumptions, explore uncharted territories, and envision new ways to fulfill your mission.

Customer-Centric Innovation: Listen deeply to your audience. Understand their evolving needs and aspirations. Use your purpose as a springboard to create innovative solutions that resonate profoundly with them.

Collaborative Innovation: Embrace the power of collaboration. Seek partnerships with like-minded organizations, entrepreneurs, and creatives who share your brand's purpose. Together, you can amplify your impact and inspire groundbreaking ideas.

Persona: The Dynamic Connection

Your brand's persona is the bridge to your audience—the embodiment of their characteristics, desires, and aspirations. It's a fluid and evolving relationship that demands continuous innovation to remain authentic and relevant.

Tips for Audience-Centric Innovation:

Stay Agile: Keep a finger on the pulse of your audience. Monitor shifts in behavior, preferences, and trends. Adapt your messaging and offerings accordingly to maintain relevance.

Empathetic Engagement: Deepen your understanding of your audience's experiences and challenges. Use this empathy to drive innovation in your products, services, and communication strategies.

Feedback-Driven Evolution: Encourage feedback from your audience and internal teams. Use this input to refine your brand persona, ensuring it resonates with your audience's evolving values and aspirations.

Innovating within the realms of purpose and persona is a continuous journey. By nurturing purpose-driven innovation and embracing audience-centric creativity, your brand can transcend the ordinary, connecting profoundly with your audience and driving transformative change in the world. It's not just a conclusion; it's a new beginning for your brand's extraordinary future.

Personality: The Human Heartbeat

In the heartbeat of your brand, there is a rhythm—a distinctive personality that sets the tone for all your interactions. Paired with this heartbeat is your brand's proclamation, the narrative that gives it a voice, purpose, and meaning. Together, these pillars bring a human touch to your brand, forging connections that resonate with your audience's emotions and intellect.

Tips for Cultivating Your Brand's Human Heartbeat:

Periodic Personality Check-Ups: Just as humans grow and change, your brand's personality can evolve. Periodically assess if it aligns with your audience's sentiments and your brand's core values. Innovation in personality might involve subtle shifts or transformative changes.

Empathetic Evolution: Listen to your audience's evolving needs and desires. A brand with a human heartbeat shows empathy by adapting to meet these changing expectations while staying true to its essence.

Diverse Collaboration: Seek collaboration with diverse voices and perspectives. These creative partnerships can infuse fresh life into your brand's personality, fostering growth through creative diversity.

Proclamation: Crafting a Resonant Voice

Your brand's proclamation is more than words; it's the voice that narrates your journey, beliefs, and significance. It's a powerful storytelling tool that connects with your audience on an emotional and intellectual level. Crafting a resonant proclamation is essential for keeping your brand's voice engaging and meaningful.

Tips for Crafting a Resonant Brand Proclamation:

Evolving Storytelling: Innovation in proclamation involves exploring new storytelling techniques. Experiment with interactive narratives, user-generated content, or immersive experiences to captivate and engage your audience.

Purpose-Driven Messaging: Infuse your brand's purpose into your proclamation. Create messages that motivate action, inspire advocacy, and invite participation, effectively propelling your mission forward.

Real-Time Engagement: Embrace real-time marketing and proclamation. Stay agile and responsive to current events and trends, allowing your brand to engage with its audience in relevant and innovative ways.

Picture your brand as a ship sailing through the vast sea of the market. In this vast expanse, brand positioning acts as your reliable compass, guiding your way through the turbulent waters of competition. It's about finding your unique place, setting your brand apart, and creating a brand positioning statement that succinctly captures your essence. Anchored in a profound understanding of your audience and the competitive landscape, your positioning charts the course towards brand distinction.

Tips for Navigating the Market Landscape:

Continuous Competitor Analysis: Innovate in your market navigation by adopting a proactive stance on competitor analysis. Regularly assess your competitors' strategies, and leverage these insights to identify gaps and opportunities in your positioning.

Dynamic Positioning: Recognize that markets evolve, and so should your positioning. Regularly revisit and adapt your brand's position to remain relevant and competitive. Innovate by aligning your positioning with emerging trends and shifting consumer sentiments.

Audience-Centric Positioning: Consider innovative approaches to align your brand positioning with your audience's evolving needs and aspirations. Dive deep into your audience's psyche to understand their changing preferences, and adjust your positioning accordingly. Innovate by fostering a sense of belonging and relevance in their lives.

Presence: A Seamless Connection

In a world where attention spans are fleeting and choices abound, your brand presence acts as the bridge between you and your audience. It's about crafting a seamless, engaging, and memorable experience across all touchpoints. Whether it's your website, social media, or in-person interactions, your brand presence defines the essence of your connection with your audience.

Tips for Building a Seamless Brand Presence:

Multi-Sensory Engagement: Innovate your brand presence by engaging multiple senses. Consider how your brand can evoke emotions not only visually but also through sound, touch, taste, and smell, depending on your industry and audience.

Data-Driven Personalization: Embrace data-driven personalization to create tailored experiences. Leverage data analytics to understand your audience's behavior and preferences. Use this information to innovate your presence by delivering customized content and interactions.

Unified Cross-Platform Consistency: Innovate your brand presence by ensuring consistency across all platforms. Develop guidelines that harmonize your messaging, aesthetics, and user experience, creating a unified brand identity. This consistency enhances recognition and trust among your audience, fostering a lasting connection.

Performance: Exceptional Brand Experiences

Picture your brand as a grand symphony, where every note and every instrument represents a unique customer touchpoint. At the intersection of these interactions and experiences lies your brand's performance, a harmonious orchestration of every customer engagement, from the crescendo of exceptional customer service to the delicate nuances of product quality. It's a symphony where your brand takes center stage, captivating its audience and leaving them with an unforgettable experience.

Tips for Elevating Brand Performance:

Audience-Oriented Composition: To create a performance that resonates deeply, compose your brand's interactions with an acute focus on your audience's needs and desires. Conduct in-depth audience research to uncover the melodies that will strike a chord with them. Innovate by anticipating their preferences and weaving them into every brand note.

Value-Driven Arrangements: Craft your brand performance around the central theme of value delivery. Each interaction should be an opportunity to enrich your audience's lives, whether through solving their problems or fulfilling their desires. Innovate by constantly seeking new ways to enhance the value you provide.

Trust-Building Crescendos: Trust is the cornerstone of a memorable brand performance. Every touchpoint should be orchestrated to instill confidence in your brand. Consistently deliver on your promises and exceed expectations to build a crescendo of trust that resounds with your audience. Innovate by integrating transparency and authenticity into your brand's performance, fostering deeper connections.

The Unbreakable Connection: Shared Values and Experiences

In the heart of your brand, an unbreakable connection is forged with your audience—a connection grounded in shared values and experiences. Beyond aesthetics and transactions, your brand becomes an embodiment of purpose and resonance, fostering a deep and lasting connection.

Throughout the chapters of this journey into the world of branding, we've uncovered a treasure trove of insights. We've explored the art of crafting a compelling brand proclamation that authentically tells your story and connects with your audience. We've delved into the nuances of brand personality, understanding that your brand, much like a person, can resonate deeply with individuals through archetypal characteristics. The significance of brand positioning has become evident, guiding your brand's path in the vast sea of the market. We've seen how brand performance is the culmination of every customer touchpoint, an opportunity to create exceptional experiences.

However, it's not just the individual elements but the interplay between them that truly weaves the tapestry of your brand. Purpose and persona give birth to an authentic and relatable core, while personality and proclamation breathe life into it. Positioning and presence set the stage, and performance brings the narrative to life. In this intricate dance, an unbreakable connection emerges, where your brand and your audience become partners in a meaningful journey.

The Framework for a Future of Impact

Today's competitive landscape demands more than a superficial brand identity; it calls for purpose-driven branding. By embracing the framework outlined in this journey, you have laid the foundation for a brand that transcends the ordinary. It's a brand that doesn't merely seek attention but commands admiration, not just transactions but genuine connection.

In this culmination of purpose, persona, personality, proclamation, positioning, presence, and performance, you have unlocked the potential to create a brand that stands as a beacon of change, resonating with your audience and propelling your mission forward. The lessons learned, the strategies employed, and the insights uncovered throughout this book provide you with the tools to shape your brand's destiny.

Now, as you embark on this new chapter in your brand's journey, remember that the power to make a profound impact lies within your hands. Harness the unique character of your brand, the authenticity of your story, and the unwavering dedication to your purpose. Engage with your audience on a deeper level, and let your brand be a force for positive change.

With this framework as your guide, you have the means to not only thrive in the competitive landscape but to shine as a beacon of inspiration and transformation. Your brand is no longer just a name or logo; it's a catalyst for change, a symbol of purpose, and a vehicle for impact.

It's time to step boldly into the future, armed with the knowledge and insights you've gained on this journey. Your brand's destiny is waiting to be written, and its story is one of purpose, resonance, and lasting impact. Take the first step, and let your brand become a powerful force for change and a source of inspiration for generations to come.

Meet Joi M. Sears, a Creative Strategist, Brand Designer, and Social Entrepreneur. With a passion for the art of branding, she has spent years delving into the intricate dance between design and purpose. Her journey through the ever-evolving world of branding has been an adventure marked by a dedication to crafting unique narratives and impactful designs.

Having walked the fine line between creativity and strategy, Joi brings a wealth of experience to the table. With a background steeped in the arts and a masterful understanding of the human psyche, she has developed a knack for turning brands into compelling stories that resonate deeply with audiences.

Joi is not just an author; she's a brand magician, weaving spells with color palettes, fonts, and imagery that capture the essence of every enterprise she touches. Her commitment to conscious branding has resulted in transformative experiences for countless clients and organizations.

When Joi isn't shaping the brands of tomorrow, you'll find her exploring the realms of creativity, seeking fresh inspiration, and pushing the boundaries of what's possible in the world of design. Join her on a journey through the pages of "Brand Alchemy: The Art and Design of Conscious Branding," and discover the magic that happens when passion, purpose, and branding converge.

Ready to turn theory into action? Check out this exclusive Branding Toolkit! Discover a collection of valuable resources, templates, and a free Branding Worksheet that will help you put the strategies and insights from this book into practice.

Access these essential resources by scanning the QR code below.

It's time to bring your brand vision to life.

www.ingramcontent.com/pod-product-compliance
Lightning Source LLC
Chambersburg PA
CBHW072207290526
45794CB00004B/1681